INNOVATION IN EDUCATION

LESSONS FROM PIONEERS
AROUND THE WORLD

CHARLES LEADBEATER

PHOTOGRAPHS BY ROMAIN STAROS STAROPOLI

Bloomsbury Qatar Foundation Publishing
Qatar Foundation
Villa 3, Education City
PO Box 5825
Doha, Qatar
www.bqfp.com.qa
—
Copyright
© Qatar Foundation 2012
—
The moral right of the author
has been asserted.
—
Hardback ISBN 978 99921 94 41 6
Paperback ISBN 978 99921 94 44 7
—
Cover and design by
des Signes, Paris
—
All photographs are by
Romain Staros Staropoli
—
—
Cover picture
Children at a Nanhi Kali programme
school, Mumbai, India

CONTENTS

13
FOREWORD

15
ACKNOWLEDGEMENTS

17
CHAPTER 1 | **THE BASICS: HOPE AND FRUSTRATION**

29
CHAPTER 2 | **THE PIONEERS: THE ROAD TO HIGH IMPACT**

41
CHAPTER 3 | **SCHOOLS: ESSENTIAL BUT NOT ENOUGH**

49
CHAPTER 4 | **WHO: OVERCOMING BARRIERS TO ACCESS**

69
CHAPTER 5 | **HOW: MAKING LEARNING MEANINGFUL**

83
CHAPTER 6 | **WHAT: KNOWLEDGE AND CAPABILITIES**

95
CHAPTER 7 | **WHY: COMPELLING NOT COMPULSORY**

107
CHAPTER 8 | **THE COMBINATION: MORE, BETTER AND DIFFERENT**

113
CHAPTER 9 | **INSPIRATION IN THE MARGINS**

127
CHAPTER 10 | **WE ARE A MOVEMENT**

137
CHAPTER 11 | **THE CLASH: WHEN MOVEMENTS MEET SYSTEMS**

147
CHAPTER 12 | **OPENING THE DOOR TO INFINITY**

154
BIBLIOGRAPHY

156
APPENDIX | CASE STUDIES & LINKS

157
APPENDIX | HIGH IMPACT INNOVATORS AT A GLANCE

158
INDEX

"It opened a door for me. The door is to infinity... Education does not mean getting a certificate. Education means I have the right to learn anything in this world and nothing can obstruct me"

—
A student in Bangladesh
on what using MIT's OpenCourseWare
means to him.

FOREWORD

H.E. Sheikh Abdulla bin Ali Al-Thani, PhD, Chairman
of the World Innovation Summit for Education (WISE);
President of Hamad Bin Khalifa University;
and Vice President, Education, Qatar Foundation
—

When Her Highness Sheikha Moza bint Nasser, Chairperson of the Qatar Foundation for Education, Science and Community Development, asked us some three years ago to launch an international, multi-sectoral initiative aimed at upgrading education for all, we knew it was an ambitious but vitally important mission.

Throughout most of history, education has been the preserve of the few. As a result, regrettably, only a small part of our collective potential has been put to use. Today's rapid social, economic and technological developments have brought us to a point where education should no longer be seen as a privilege, but as a prerequisite to a decent quality of life – for individuals and communities, in developed and developing countries. In short, it is a passport both to inclusion and to opportunity.

Unfortunately, education systems have not always managed to adapt. Too often our children enter adulthood without the tools that will empower them to cope with an uncertain future. Incremental change is no longer sufficient – transformational leadership is required. Our challenge is to move in that direction, working within the wide range of circumstances that prevail, while respecting and nurturing the rich diversity of cultures that are our shared heritage.

These same global processes also offer tremendous opportunities – to connect and network, to share ideas and best practices. The World Innovation Summit for Education (WISE) aims to seize that opportunity by offering a global platform for collaborative action, using innovation as a key ingredient.

Since the launch of WISE, we have been immensely heartened to discover many real-life success stories, sometimes in the most unexpected places. We knew from the outset that, in building the future of education, we must start from those initiatives that are already making a positive difference.

Since 2009, the WISE Awards have identified, showcased and promoted annually six of the most innovative and promising educational projects around the world.

These projects, and others, are beacons of hope which, given the right conditions, might grow and converge into the education revolution that we need and which people around the world are yearning for. It is the strategy of WISE to create an environment in which this can happen.

In *Innovation in Education: Lessons from Pioneers around the World*, we have visited exciting educational projects that are achieving results, often in difficult circumstances. The individuals engaged in these projects – educators and organisers – are devoting their talents and energies to giving the next generation a better start. They are true heroes of our time, and I salute and thank them for their work, and for their cooperation in helping us compile this unique guide to breakthrough educational initiatives.

I also thank the WISE Qatar Foundation team and our partner organisations for their support, and the entire WISE community, whose combined experience, talent and passion will, I am confident, engender many great things in the years to come.

I hope that this book will raise awareness of one of the most significant issues of our age, that all who care about our shared future will be able to draw encouragement from these examples, and that it will inspire original thinking and concerted action both at the grassroots level and among policy-makers.

—
Find out more about the WISE initiative
and join our growing online community at:
www.wise-qatar.org

For Diogo Vasconcelos (1968-2011),
my friend and collaborator
who died while I was in Paraguay
researching this book.

ACKNOWLEDGEMENTS

This book could not have been put together in so short a time, and to such high standards of production, without the help and commitment of many people. It would have been impossible without the tireless, resourceful research of Kathleen Stokes, who not only undertook extensive desk research but also, at short notice, plunged into field trips to the Netherlands, India and the Middle East, deploying her considerable language skills. Scores of people across the world generously gave their time to show us where they lived, went to school, worked and learned, from fathers' groups in Istanbul to the favelas of Bogotá, rural villages in India and Uganda to inner city programmes in Canada and the United States and farm schools in Paraguay. Without the generosity of our pioneers in sharing their experiences and ideas, this book would have been impossible. We have also drawn on the work of many other writers on education and innovation whose ideas we have built on: we hope we have given them due credit. My family very patiently put up with me being away for large parts of 2011.

Dr Abdulla bin Ali Al-Thani, chairman of the WISE initiative, provided invaluable support for this project. Our main thanks go to Her Highness Sheikha Moza bint Nasser. The World Innovation Summit for Education (WISE) is an initiative of Qatar Foundation for Education, Science and Community Development and was launched in 2009 at the instigation of Her Highness. This book and all the work that flows from it would have been impossible without her commitment to leading the search for innovation that can improve education around the world.

—

CHARLES LEADBEATER

THE BASICS: HOPE AND FRUSTRATION

A student from the African Institute of Mathematical Sciences looks out from the beach near the Institute's home at Muizenberg, just outside Cape Town

If you look closely at this host of children gathered around their teacher at the Kinyateke Primary School in deepest rural Uganda, you may spot a future doctor, teacher, engineer, artist, writer or businesswoman. We know there could be an aspiring mathematician hidden in that crowd because Angelina Lutambi came from a village just like this in nearby Tanzania.

"To afford the uniform, books and fees charged by state schools the entire family needed to pick cotton."

Angelina's parents were illiterate. But that did not stop Angelina's father from being determined that his bright little daughter would go to school. It was not easy. The Lutambi family were poor as poor could be. To afford the uniform, books and fees charged by state schools the entire family needed to pick cotton. When there was a drought, and so no cotton, there could be no school. Even when there was cotton to be picked there might be no teacher at the impoverished school that Angelina would walk hours to get to.

But Angelina persisted and eventually the immense natural talent of the girl from a mud hut next to the lake was spotted. After taking a degree at Dar es Salam University Anglina won one of the few available places at the African Institute for Mathematical Sciences (AIMS) in Cape Town.

Angelina prospered, focussing on the links between maths and epidemiology. She studied for a masters at Stellenbosch University in South Africa and worked for a health research organisation in Tanzania before going to Switzerland, to start a PhD. When her doctorate is completed she plans to return to her homeland to pick up her health research.

AIMS is a system for spotting and developing talent. That should be how all education systems see their task. Most do the job poorly, if at all. For the children of Kasese district in western Uganda, the struggle to get their talents recognised has recently become a little easier. They have a better school these days due to one of the remarkable projects profiled in this book – Rewrite the Future – a Save the Children campaign that has improved education for about 10m children in conflict zones in more than twenty countries. It has done this by building the equivalent of two schools a day for five years.

If education can find talent in the most unlikely places then it can also bring hope to the most unpromising places – places like La Capilla.

Emmanuel Kambale, the headmaster of Kinyateke Primary School in Uganda, surrounded by his pupils

Twenty-five minutes' drive south of the Colombian capital of Bogotá, La Capilla is part of the vast favela system known as Cazuco, the place where the poorest people live, the most recent arrivals from the countryside. La Capilla clings to a narrow strip of land, squeezed between a mud cliff and factories that line the main road out of the city. The factories belch fumes into the slum and each year the mud cliff delivers mudslides that carry away many of the feeble dwellings below. Most people in La Capilla make their living in Bogotá's vast informal economy. Gangs that peddle drugs are ever present in these favelas, as is the violence that goes with them. The community clusters around a few small shops, a DVD store, a cyber café, the church and a feeding station run by a Catholic charity which dispenses 500 lunches a day to hungry children. Everything in La Capilla is insecure, from the way people make their living to the earth beneath their feet. There cannot be many harder places to grow up. This is the place that Diego and Fabian Valendra, brothers, sixteen and fifteen, call home.

"To achieve real change we need to transform the lives of millions of children in this way, bit by bit, to make great things happen through many, many small things."

Diego and Fabian have seen their home swept away by mudslides twice and people lying murdered in the road outside. They live in a tiny house with seven other members of their family and share a room with their older sister. When other children their age were settling into school Diego and Fabian were out selling anything they could – flowers, chewing gum – in the bars of downtown Bogotá. Their working day started at 6pm and ended at four in the morning. It did not take long for them to become hooked on drugs, which they consumed with abandon.

How do you bring hope to boys like Diego and Fabian in a desperate place like La Capilla?

It's a trick Luizdary Brojas knows how to pull off. In 2003 Brojas started "learning circles" in La Capilla, based on the Escuela Nueva model of collaborative learning that Vicky Colbert first developed in rural schools in Colombia in the 1980s. Learning circles apply Escuela Nueva's core principles – collaborative and self-paced learning – to the most vulnerable city children who are at risk of slipping out of the school system.

Brojas, a tall, calm and warm woman, found Diego and Fabian, both made ill by the drugs they were taking, playing on scrubland that passes for a park. She asked whether they wanted to join the circle. They were worried they would need official papers, books and money: "You just have to be clean," she told them.

At the outset the children, who had been exposed to violence from an early age, fought a lot. Brojas explained: "What these children miss is the magic hand of love and affection, to make them feel valued. If you can start looking at each one of them individually you can start to see their potential and then it becomes easier to work with them. But you cannot teach them in the traditional way. You have to work with them and get them to work together. The way they learn to form relationships with one another is key."

The learning circle seems to have changed Diego and Fabian. They are in school, a year behind their peers, but determined to catch up and keen to stick the course. "We have to sit in rows, with the teacher at the front," Diego explained. "In the circle we all sat around together, with the teacher in the circle. But what we learned about how to get on with one another has been important. We want to stick it out, to get a career, to help our family."

For Brojas the change was even more fundamental: "Diego and Fabian fell in love with life again, they dared to have dreams again. To achieve real change we need to transform the lives of millions of children in this way, bit by bit, to make great things happen through many, many small things."

Angelina's story tells us that talent can be found anywhere if only we know how to look. Diego and Fabian's story tells us hope can be generated anywhere if people can learn in the right way. Azize Sagir and Ceren Can Seren's story tells us that education can generate its own momentum by raising people's expectations of what is possible.

Azize Sagir is intent and alert, sitting on a simple sofa in her bare apartment in the Istanbul suburb of Esenler Merkez. She puts a protective arm around her four-year-old son Samet to encourage him to complete the worksheet that sits in front of them on a low table. He concentrates hard, keen to impress his mother; she responds by gently praising his efforts. The worksheet comes from a programme Azize has enlisted in with about twenty other young mothers, to prepare their children to go to school.

CLOCKWISE FROM TOP LEFT: Luizdary Brojas with some of her students in La Capilla, Bogotá; Vicky Colbert, the founder of Escuela Neuva, in her office; Diego and Fabian Valendra listening to Vicky Colbert; background material on Escuela Neuava; Diego near his home in La Capilla; the view over the favela towards downtown Bogotá; two boys near the feeding station in La Capilla run by a Catholic charity that caters for hundreds of children each day

ABOVE: Azize Sagir, with her husband Cengiiz and son Samet, in their apartment in Esenler Merkez, Istanbul; **ABOVE LEFT:** Samet reading at home; **LEFT:** Azize leading her son through one of the exercises provided by MOCEP; **BELOW:** Azize, (second left) in her local mothers' group; **FAR LEFT:** Muzzuz Olcay, the group's facilitator; **BELOW LEFT:** A mother from the group. Most grew up in the countryside with limited education

Azize grew up in a remote Anatolian village, one of five siblings, and left school at the age of twelve to work in a market garden: "I would like to have gone to school but that wasn't an option. I had to work in the garden." Her frustration has turned into an implacable determination that her own children will not suffer a similar fate, their own potential stunted. Gesturing to the photographs of Samet's elder sisters she declared: "God willing they will both go to secondary school. Yes I have a lot of dreams for them. I want them to have their own vocation and occupation. I do not want them to have to be dependent upon their husbands."

That ambition leads Azize each week to the cramped, windowless back room of a local community centre, where with a group of other mothers, over about six months, she will learn how to prepare Samet to hold a pencil, make his letters, count in tens. The group, deftly led by veteran facilitator Muzzuz Olcay, alternates between mocking laughter at tales of their husbands' antics and fierce concentration as they hang onto Olcay's tips. Not a single mother went to school beyond the age of twelve. All are determined to give their own children a better chance in life.

Ceren Can Seren is proof that their ambitions are realistic. In 1983 she was at a pre-school group, attached to the Eczacibasi pharmaceuticals factory in Istanbul, which employed her mother, where the pilot for what became the Mother Child Education Program (MOCEP) was launched. Ceren's mother was obsessed with educating her daughter even in the face of outright scepticism from her relatives who could see little point in educating a girl. Thanks to her mother's efforts, supported by MOCEP, Ceren was the first in her school class to read and she never looked back. Her teachers, she says, showed her "a different path to walk in life".

After leaving school with flying colours, Ceren took two degrees and now works as an architect in a thriving practice serving Istanbul's commercial property boom. When she is ready she will set up her own business. She was not prepared to be so patient as far as her own daughter's education was concerned.

With 35 other parents Ceren has set up her own pre-school, The Little Black Fish, modelled on Montessori principles. She explained: "I want a school that will preserve my child's spirit and keep alive what is inside. That is a proper education." She wants something that will find and nurture her daughter's talents.

Azize and Ceren are just tiny particles in a mushrooming cloud of rising expectations. All over the world parents are determined to give their children a better start in life. Children are hungry to learn and express themselves. For women like Ceren and Azize it is not just about lessons and exams; it is about women claiming the power to shape their own lives.

The mathematician from a mud hut in Tanzania. The boys from the Bogotá slum who want a career. The young woman, the first in her family to complete secondary school, who has set up a school for her daughters. What do these stories tell us about the state of education around the world?

────────────────────────

The first thing they tell us is that hundreds of millions of families send their children to school every day in the hope that education will change their lives for the better.

Education plays a vital role in economic development, by providing skills and knowledge to make the economy more productive. Many families see in education qualifications that will lead their children to better jobs and higher incomes. Yet the benefits extend well beyond the economic. Education is generative: it brings multiple benefits to people and over a very long time. In rural Pakistan the gains might show up first in improved hygiene, which leads to better family health. In India it might be in the way young women are deciding to continue learning even after they get married. In zones of conflict, education can provide people with something in common, which helps overcome religious and ethnic differences. In Colombia, Escuela Nueva's collaborative learning does not just educate children in maths and Spanish, but in how to govern themselves, to become citizens.

For these people education is not just about exams and qualifications. It offers them the hope that their place in society will not be fixed by where they were born. People believe that through education they can remake their lives; talent can be found anywhere, hope kindled in the harshest places. Expectations of what education can and should offer are constantly rising.

The second message, however, is that education can also deliver disappointment and frustration.

It's not good enough to get more children into school, if few of them learn and what they learn

"I want a school that will preserve my child's spirit and keep alive what is inside. That is a proper education."

makes little difference to their lives. As Vicky Colbert, the founder of Escuela Nueva, puts it: "Education is the best hope we have for creating fairness and social justice, but only education of the right kind will do that."

For all the hope that it excites, schooling can be rigid and bureaucratic, conservative and inflexible, resistant to new ideas and difficult to reform. That inability to adapt means that education, far from delivering social mobility, can entrench social inequality. Education can become a process for sorting children into those that will go on to university and into the professions, from those who fall behind and drop out of systems that almost seem designed to make life difficult for them. For too many families, in both the developed and the developing world, demography is destiny: where you come from, the family you are born into, will determine whether you go to a decent school that will shape your life chances. Inflexible, impersonal and rigid systems and rote learning are likely to reinforce rather than break through inequalities of class, caste and gender.

> "The status quo can be changed but it takes a lot of outrage and a lot of good examples."

Just as expectations of education are rising around the world, so is evidence of disappointment.

In most countries of the world, most children are now enrolled in primary schools that are free and accessible to most families. You might think that if children can go to school to be taught by a well-trained teacher, the rest should pretty much take care of itself. If only it were so simple.

The UN Millennium Development Goals, in order to ensure that by 2015 all girls and boys are able to complete a full course of primary education, have encouraged a huge government push to universalise primary education. In India 95% of children have a state primary school within half a mile of where they live. In several African states – Uganda, Kenya and Ghana– children flocked to school after primary education was made free. According to UNICEF, between 1999 and 2006 primary enrolments in Sub-Saharan Africa rose from 54% to 70%, while in East and South Asia they rose from 75% to 88%. Worldwide the number of children of primary school age who were out of school dropped from 103m in 1999 to 73m in 2006. More children also have access to secondary school despite it being more expensive. Between 1995 and 2008 gross secondary school enrolment ratios in Sub-Saharan African rose from 25% to 34%, in South Asia they rose from 44% to 51% and in East Asia from 64% to 74%. Over the past 50 years the number of students enrolled in secondary school increased tenfold to 500m.

Yet the fact that children are enrolled in school does not, necessarily, mean they are being taught. The 2002 and 2006 World Absenteeism Survey conducted by the World Bank found that public school teachers in countries such as Bangladesh, Ecuador, Indonesia and Peru miss one day in five. In India, when inspectors made unannounced visits they found 50% of teachers drinking tea, reading the newspaper or chatting to colleagues. It should be no surprise that many children do not learn what they are supposed to have been taught. A survey by Pratham, India's leading educational NGO, found that only 35% of children in sixth grade could read a story and only 30% could do maths calculations designed for children in second grade. The frustration and disappointment bred by these systems can lead to dropouts and exam failures.

In West Bengal, for example, only 17 of 100 students starting primary education will make it to their school leaving exams. India produces more engineers than anywhere in the world; it also produces more school dropouts. By the turn of the twentieth century all Brazilian children had a place at school. The illiteracy rate among 14-year-olds has fallen to 2.5%. Girls have access to education on the same basis as boys. Yet one study found that half the resources of Brazilian education are spent on pupils repeating grades. Those falling behind and dropping out come disproportionately from the poorer sections of society. In Kenya, following the phased abolition of school entrance fees, enrolments reached 100% in 2003, rising from 5.9m in 2002 to 7.6m in 2005. Rising enrolments, however, have dramatically increased class sizes in state systems strapped for resources. A study of 210 primary schools in Western Kenya in 2007 found the average class size was 83, and 28% of first-grade classes had more than 100 pupils. A UNESCO review in 2006 found that less than half of those that enrol for primary school in Kenya complete all eight years.

This litany of disappointment is not confined to the developing world. In the United Kingdom 30,000 children a year leave the school system with few qualifications. In France the failures are most evident in the high rates of grade repetitions and dropouts among children from poorer suburbs with large ethnic minorities. Perhaps the most glaring example is the United States.

In the United States, spending per child in education rose by 70% in the 25 years to 2010 but produced no appreciable improvement in literacy rates. In 1969 about 77% of high school students graduated within four years. By the year 2000, that had fallen to 69%. The US public school system caters particularly poorly for children from ethnic minority and immigrant backgrounds who will make up a majority of the US population within the next three decades. Most of those immigrants will be from Mexico, Latin America, Asia and Africa. American public schools are serving an increasingly diverse population in which many parents have limited experience of formal schooling and many families do not speak English as their first language. Yet these are precisely the students that are most likely to fail. As Linda Darling-Hammond explains in *The Flat World and Education*, too many of the poorest children go to schools with fewer resources and less-qualified teachers, where they have fewer opportunities for challenging and exciting learning tailored to their needs and the pace at which they learn.

The frustrations people feel with traditional schooling are only likely to intensify as schools fail to deliver the kinds of skills needed in a modern, innovative economy. Schools that teach children to get through tests will not impart the social and entre-preneurial skills they will need to prosper at work. Even when schools are hitting the target they may still miss the point. The main focus of education policy globally has been to get more children into better schools. In the decades to come the focus will have to shift, to make sure children have ample opportunities to learn: before they go to school, when they are at school and outside school. Too many children cannot get to a school, but just as many children are in school and learning too little.

The third lesson from our three success stories is that under the right circumstances a mix of hope and frustration can provide the fuel for innovation, and lead to the creation of more effective solutions.

Innovators meet frustration not with complaints, but with a commitment to devise more effective solutions. But this often requires innovators to break with conventional thinking and challenge orthodox models. As Bill Gates, Microsoft's founder, put it in an interview for the film *Waiting for Superman*: "The status quo can be changed but it takes a lot of outrage and a lot of good examples." In each of these three stories an innovator created a good example of a different way to learn.

Angelina, the mathematician of our first story, was lucky to go to AIMS, which has broken with the traditional model of university lectures to create a unique, collaborative and interactive approach to learning. Diego and Fabian are among the many millions of children in Latin America who have benefited from Escuela Nueva's methods enabling children to learn together, at their own pace, from one another, in circles, as an alternative to classrooms in which children sit in rows, parroting what a teacher tells them. Azize Sagir's son is benefiting from an innovation that trains mothers to become the first educators of their children, instead of relying on professionals who, in developing countries, are often too scarce and costly.

Innovation can cut through the inertia that envelops many school systems by mobilising three key ingredients: the rising hopes and expectations of millions of parents and children; mounting frustration with the shortcomings of traditional models of education; and a commitment to develop new and more effective solutions. When these three – hope, frustration and experimentation – come together in the right way they can produce radical innovation that delivers much better outcomes for families, at affordable costs and on a large scale. Understanding where that kind of innovation comes from is the purpose of this book.

This is not a scientific, academic study of innovation. Nor is it a set of cookie-cutter recipes for people to follow. The focus is on the work of 16 pioneers around the world who have developed new and more effective approaches to education that work at scale. These pioneers are almost all drawn from applicants for awards from the World Innovation Summit for Education (WISE) in 2009 and 2010. By tracing the story of how these pioneering innovations came about, developed, spread and acquired scale we hope to raise awareness of why innovation in education is needed, where it comes from and how more can be generated.

First we introduce our 16 pioneers and the innovations they have created, starting with five friends from Karachi who had a crazy idea.

Children heading to school in Bhimavaram, Andhra Pradesh. Though enrolments have increased, 72m children in India are still not at school

Classroom in Kallakuru village primary school, West Godavari district, Andhra Pradesh, India. Children take turns making crafts and artwork while waiting to use the Telugu-based Bridges to the Future software implemented as part of the Model Schools programme of the Byrraju Foundation

CHAPTER 2

THE PIONEERS: THE ROAD TO HIGH IMPACT

Girls at primary school in Juvvalapalem village, West Godavari district in India which uses Bridges to the Future's Telugu language educational software as part of the Byrraju Foundation's Model Schools programme

"A drop of perfume in a bucket of water can fragrance an entire room."

An old Pakistani proverb

On 14 August 1995 a group of five friends met in Karachi to celebrate the anniversary of Pakistan's independence. It did not take long for the conversation to turn to the ills of their country, which was beset by a spate of violent kidnappings. The five, all successful businessmen and professionals, soon grew tired of their own complaints. They decided they needed to take action. They discussed setting up a volunteer police force or launching a health initiative. Finally they hit upon an idea that everyone liked: they would build 1,000 high quality schools for the poorest children in Pakistan.

When they asked leading educationalists for advice they were given a frosty reception and told to stick to what they knew best. Undeterred, they persisted, armed with a few clear principles. They would build schools all over the country that would serve girls and boys in equal numbers. The buildings would be solid but attractive, light and airy. The teachers would be properly trained, well-managed and held accountable for their performance. Parents would pay fees they could afford. The money to fund the schools would come from donations from many sources. The foundation they would set up to fund the schools would not bear the name of any of their families. In honour of the people they were serving it would be called The Citizens Foundation (TCF).

Innovation rarely runs smoothly, and it did not take long for them to run into their first obstacle. Mushtaq Chhapra, one of the founding group and now the Foundation's president and chief executive officer, recalled: "These illiterate parents in slum area of Karachi where we were setting up our first school said they would never send their daughters to a school with male teachers." It came as a shock. For a time it seemed that their goal of providing co-educational schools would fall by the wayside. Then they figured out a solution: they would employ only women teachers.

From those first five schools around Karachi, in 1995, The Citizens Foundation has blossomed. By 2011 it was running 730 schools, with 102,000 students, employing 5,400 female teachers, all of them driven to school in small mini-buses to ensure their safety. Each teacher gets 100 hours of training before they start work, from a team of 60 master trainers that TCF has created from amongst its own best teachers.

In many parts of the world, providing children with trained teachers, who come to school every day to work in light, airy, well-built schools, teaching classes of no more than 30, with equal numbers of girls and boys, might not seem like an innovation. But in the context of Pakistan's failing state education system The Citizens Foundation's schools are hugely innovative.

A third of primary-age children in Pakistan do not go to school. Six in ten schools have no electricity and a third have neither water nor latrines. Each day a quarter of Pakistan's teachers do not turn up for work. Not surprisingly perhaps, only 1 in 100 children who start kindergarten finish their studies in Year 12. In Citizens Foundation schools 73% of children go on to study in Year 11 and 12. It is little short of a revolution.

only 1 in 100 children who start kindergarten finish their studies in Year 12.

The Citizens Foundation has innovated new approaches to learning, introduced classes in critical thinking and has its own educational philosophy organised around conceptual knowledge, communication skills, creative thinking, confidence and core values. Yet in truth the foundation has not created a radically different alternative to government schools, as much as shown how they could be made massively more effective. Even when The Citizens Foundation reaches its goal of 1,000 schools, which it should in 2015, that will account for less than 0.5% of school age children in Pakistan. What difference can it really make?

As Chhapra explains, TCF's impact extends far beyond its own schools: "Now we've been going for a few years we've started to see real change in the communities we serve. Homes are cleaner. Parents are more interested. When the nation erupted in violence after the assassination of Benazir Bhutto communities rallied to defend our schools against looters. But we cannot make change on our own. We have to influence the government system." The Citizens Foundation is the drop of fragrance in the bucket.

The Foundation is a prime example of high impact innovation and why it matters so much. Already one of the most populous young countries in the world, with a population of 180m, by mid-century Pakistan's population will be 340m, most of it under the age of 25. Pakistan could be a thriving Islamic republic with a young, confident, well-educated and entrepreneurial population. But if it fails to create more effective ways for all its population to learn it could be home to a large, disaffected, underemployed and disenfranchised population of angry young men. As Sir Michael Barber, co-chair of the Pakistan Education Task Force, put it: "That second future would be devastating for Pakistan and deeply problematic for the global community."

All over the world people are hungry for more innovations of this kind to meet their rising expectations that their place in society is not fixed and education will improve their lives. Meeting those expectations will require many more innovations to generate better opportunities to learn for hundreds of millions of people. But what does innovation mean in the context of education?

———————————————————

Innovation is widely talked about and yet often misunderstood. It is common to think that innovation is a largely creative process, in which a lone genius invents a new technology or product, almost from scratch, working with a blank sheet of paper. The reality is that innovation is invariably a collaborative and cumulative process, often drawing on older ideas and assembling novel combinations of existing ideas. This can involve the application of entirely new technologies. Yet effective innovation, especially in services such as education, often comes from changes in how people work together. It is rare for innovations to spring to life, fully formed, with little need for refinement. Almost all really effective innovation involves extensive changes once a product starts being used, as consumers amend, adapt and add to the basic product. It took Henry Ford ten years of trial and error to hone his system for making a mass-produced, cheap car and it involved combining techniques from railroad-scheduling, meatpacking and the sewing machine industry. Many of the innovations we see today in modern cars came from adaptations made by early users, including the windscreen wiper, the glove box and the seat belt. Ford lost his leadership of the industry to General Motors, which had innovated new approaches to marketing. The US car industry in turn ceded leadership to the Japanese car companies in the 1980s, after they developed well-designed, high quality and affordable cars. In most industries innovation is an unfolding and iterative process, which often involves competition and collaboration, imitation and emulation, users as well as producers.

Innovation is needed in education to develop more effective ways for people to learn. Sometimes this might involve the application of new technologies, computers and the web, mobile phones and iPads. More often it is about people – teachers, pupils, families, friends – finding new ways to work together. It is rarely rocket science. Pockets of innovation will not be enough to meet the scale of challenge that faces Pakistan and other developing nations. They need effective, affordable, scaleable innovation that can change the way millions of people learn.

To find such high impact innovations we have examined a unique sample: 80 cases of social innovation in education from around the world. These were the projects shortlisted for awards made by the World Innovation Summit for Education (WISE) in 2009 and 2010. WISE is an initiative of Qatar Foundation for Education, Science and Community Development, launched in 2009 under the aegis of Her Highness Sheikha Moza bint Nasser, who put the aims this way: "WISE is based on the practical awareness that the challenges in education are no longer bound by countries' political boundaries and, therefore, its mandate is international. WISE recognises that the challenges facing the world community have never been greater –that we need innovative solutions not achieved by traditional approaches alone. WISE asserts that the desire to innovate is, in fact, an innate human need to shape and improve our environment." The annual WISE Summit brings together more than 1,000 recognised educational innovators from all over the world to Doha for three days to share ideas, spread best practice and learn from one another. In 2011 the WISE Prize for Education was launched, the world's first major international prize to reward individuals or teams who have made an outstanding, worldwide contribution to education. The WISE Awards scheme, from which our cases are drawn, recognises, showcases and promotes six original projects every year that demonstrate a significant impact. Our cases were drawn from the projects shortlisted for awards in 2009 and 2010, supplemented by a small number of other cases associated with the WISE initiative.

There are limitations to our approach. This is not a scientific sample, nor a randomly controlled test. The innovative activity that goes on every day within formal education systems, from policy-makers and practitioners, is probably under-represented. Some regions of the world, such as China and Central and Eastern Europe, are also not as prominent as they could be.

Yet these 80 innovative projects, from almost 40 different countries, cover almost every stage of education, from pre-school to postgraduate and teacher training. They give us an invaluable snapshot of the state of innovation in education around the world: what it is focused on, where it comes from, how it scales, where it is strong and where weak.

Sixteen of these cases are particularly interesting. They are proven innovations, which significantly improve educational outcomes. Yet they also have potential for scale because they can be replicated beyond the place where they started.

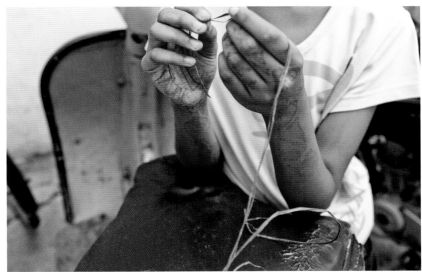

Like many in the developing world these children in Hyderabad have to apply their skills in the street as much as at school

THE SIXTEEN CASES AROUND THE WORLD

THE WEEKEND SCHOOL

The IMC Weekend School in the Netherlands is a secular Sunday school in which professionals from a wide variety of fields teach practical subjects and creative lessons to students mainly from immigrant backgrounds.

PATHWAYS TO EDUCATION

Pathways to Education is a Canadian programme that provides young people from poor inner-city neighbourhoods with new incentives and support to complete their high school education and go on to college. Pathways, which is on track to spread to 16 sites, has dramatically improved educational outcomes among the most disadvantaged communities.

REWRITE THE FUTURE

Rewrite the Future was a five-year campaign launched by Save the Children which improved education for almost 10m children in 20 conflict zones around the world.

MIT OPENCOURSEWARE

The OpenCourseWare platform launched by the Massachusetts Institute of Technology in 2001 provides free online materials for more than 2,000 courses, which have been used by 72m learners.

CRISTO REY

The Cristo Rey network in the United States is a network of 24 financially self-sufficient schools, serving poor inner-city neighbourhoods, in which the 6,400 students work a few days each month to pay for their education.

ESCUELA NUEVA

Escuela Nueva is a methodology, based on printed learning guides, to allow children to follow collaborative, self-paced approaches to learning. Escuela Nueva's methods have been adopted by 17,000 schools in Colombia and by education authorities in several other countries.

FUNDACIÓN PARAGUAYA

The San Francisco Agriculture School set up by Fundación Paraguaya in Cerrito, Paraguay, has inspired a worldwide movement of self-sufficient farm schools serving poor communities. The students grow food and run restaurants and hotels to earn the money to pay for a first class education.

APRENDIZ

Aprendiz, which started in São Paulo, Brazil, is developing ways for communities to provide richer learning opportunities outside and alongside schools. Aprendiz is one of the most influential educational NGOs in Brazil.

MOCEP

The Mother Child Education Program (MOCEP) in Turkey has trained more than 300,000 mothers to become the first educators of their children, to prepare them for school. Children of mothers who go through the programme are much more likely to go on to university or college.

WE LOVE READING

We Love Reading is a national campaign in Jordan to promote independent reading by training mothers to set up reading groups for children aged 6–12 in local mosques.

THE CITIZENS FOUNDATION

The Citizens Foundation operates 730 schools, serving more than 100,000 children, with roughly equal numbers of girls and boys, in Pakistan.

NANHI KALI

Nanhi Kali provides support for more than 70,000 girls from the very poorest homes in five states in India to ensure they do not fall behind and drop out of school.

HOLE IN THE WALL

The Hole in the Wall initiative has installed more than 500 computers across India and Africa to develop ways for children to learn, with one another and occasional adult support, but without formal teachers. So far, they have been used by about 1m children.

SHAFALLAH CENTER

The Shafallah Center in Doha, Qatar, is a state of the art campus for 600 disabled students that has become a world centre of excellence in education and disability.

AIMS

The African Institute of Mathematical Sciences (AIMS), based in Cape Town, South Africa, employs collaborative and highly interactive learning to develop the next generation of African mathematical scientists.

TESSA

The Teacher Education in Sub-Saharan Africa (TESSA) programme is a partnership between the British Open University and 12 partner organisations in Africa to use online resources to provide in-service training to more than 400,000 teachers a year, helping them to develop more imaginative teaching techniques.

To qualify for inclusion in this list of sixteen, our innovators had to satisfy two criteria:

■ **First**, the innovation must be significant: it must draw new people into learning and provide new skills, different modes of learning, and novel incentives. These schemes depart from the standard school model to reach their goal (Diagram 1). Escuela Nueva in Colombia created a new way for children to learn independently and collaboratively, in small, rural schools with one teacher and perhaps 50 children of different ages. In Uganda, Escuela Nueva's learning guides are known as "the silent teacher." Aprendiz in Brazil developed education and learning programmes so that an entire neighbourhood could be a platform for learning. The Hole in the Wall in India enabled millions of children to organise their own learning, sometimes with the support of a facilitator, using simple computer programmes. MIT pioneered the provision of free, open source courseware, with videos of lectures, so millions of teachers and students beyond the college could follow its courses. These innovations are all the more striking because of their context. The education provided in Cristo Rey's schools is in many respects unremarkable: it prepares young people to go to college. What is remarkable is that Cristo Rey has found a way to do this in the poorest inner city districts with students from immigrant families who often do not speak English and have never been near a university. What might appear to be standard practice in one setting can be highly innovative in another. Most of our high impact interventions are effective only because they have dared to challenge orthodox practice.

■ **Second**, these innovators have an impact well beyond the site where they first got started (or at least have credible plans in place) and they deliver proven benefits (Diagram 2). Rewrite The Future improved the education of about 10m children in conflict zones in 20 countries. MIT's OpenCourseWare is used by millions of independent learners each year. Millions of children have benefited from Escuela Nueva's model, which has been adopted in several other countries. The Open University's TESSA programme of open access, online teacher-training modules has been used by hundreds of thousands of teachers in Africa. Cristo Rey has grown from a single school in an inner-city neighbourhood in Chicago to a network of 24 schools across the United States. The African Institute of Mathematical Sciences, which has two campuses, one in South Africa and a second in Senegal, has well-developed plans to create a network of ten centres across the continent. The Shafallah Center in Doha is an international centre of excellence in teaching disabled children whose impact has spread as a model of excellence.

The appendix (page 157) encapsulates basic information about each of these high impact cases. In the remainder of this book we also refer to examples drawn from the larger set of 80 award nominees. But our main focus is on the lessons to be learned from these high impact innovators because they shed light on perhaps the most difficult challenge facing education systems around the world: how to develop proven innovations, which significantly improve educational outcomes, at large scale and affordable cost.

DIAGRAM 1 | **DEGREE OF INNOVATION**

High

HOLE IN THE WALL
Self-organised learning, without teachers, using computers

MIT OPENCOURSEWARE
Technology platform for open access to online courses
Shafallah, AIMS, Escuela Nueva, Aprendiz, IMC Weekend School

FUNDACIÓN PARAGUAYA/CRISTO REY
Financially self-sustaining schools.
Pupils work to afford to employ teachers

MOCEP
Groups of mothers as early educators

THE CITIZENS FOUNDATION
Female workforce to allow co-education

WE LOVE READING
Training mothers to form children's reading groups in mosques

REWRITE THE FUTURE
Getting more children in conflict zones into school

Low

DIAGRAM 2 | **REACH AND IMPACT**

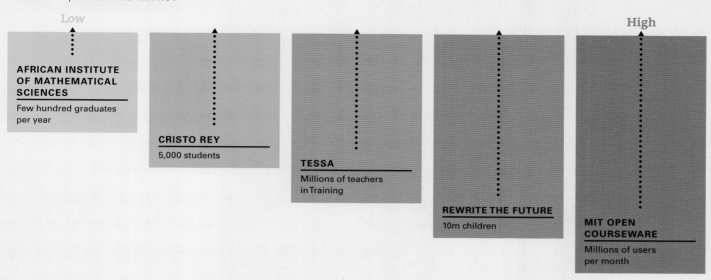

Low

High

AFRICAN INSTITUTE OF MATHEMATICAL SCIENCES

Few hundred graduates per year

CRISTO REY

5,000 students

TESSA

Millions of teachers in Training

REWRITE THE FUTURE

10m children

MIT OPEN COURSEWARE

Millions of users per month

DIAGRAM 3 | **THE HIGH IMPACT INNOVATION GRID**

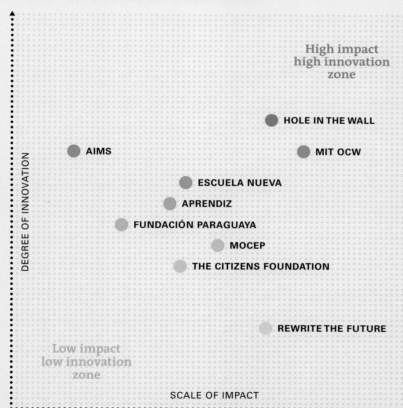

High impact high innovation zone

HOLE IN THE WALL

AIMS

MIT OCW

ESCUELA NUEVA

APRENDIZ

FUNDACIÓN PARAGUAYA

MOCEP

THE CITIZENS FOUNDATION

REWRITE THE FUTURE

Low impact low innovation zone

DEGREE OF INNOVATION

SCALE OF IMPACT

DEFINING HIGH IMPACT INNOVATION

These three diagrams convey visually the basic ingredients of our definition of high impact innovation.

Diagram 1 | **Degree of Innovation** ranks eight of the projects in terms of their degree of innovation: the extent to which they depart from the standard educational model in which teachers instruct classes in 50-minute blocks and test students in exams at the end of the course. Rewrite The Future is ranked low on the scale because its main aim was to get more children into school. Hole in the Wall is ranked high because it encourages self-organised learning using computers out of school.

Diagram 2 | **Reach and Impact** ranks the projects in terms of the number of students they reach. This takes no account of the intensity of the learning involved. The African Institute of Mathematical Sciences has the lowest reach (but with a high intensity). MIT's OpenCourseWare programme, at the other end of the scale, has reached more than 72m learners in a decade.

Diagram 3 | **The High Impact Innovation Grid** combines two dimensions to plot degree of innovation *and* scale of reach. AIMS is towards the top left because it has an innovative approach to pedagogy but low reach. Rewrite the Future is in the bottom right: it has reached millions but with fairly traditional approaches to schooling. Most of the projects cluster in the middle, combining some innovation with significant reach. Those that use technology creatively, such as Hole in the Wall and OpenCourseWare, are in the top right of the diagram because they able to combine high reach with significant innovation. These rankings are subjective, not scientific.

Classroom in Kinyateke
School, Kasese District, Uganda

CHAPTER 3

SCHOOLS: ESSENTIAL BUT NOT ENOUGH

Children outside the Kinyateke Primary School near Kasese, in Uganda, which has benefited from the Rewrite the Future programme led by Save the Children

How could five people improve the education of 8m children in just five years, working in some of the most difficult conditions imaginable, in the midst of conflict and its direct aftermath? This is how.

First of all you have to choose a really difficult place to work. Major wars between states are less common than they were but conflicts within states are far more numerous. There were 32 such conflicts in 2007 and 39 in 2010. The average civil war or regional conflict lasts at least a decade. Some conflicts, for example in Sri Lanka, drag on for thirty years, taking a toll on five or six generations. Even when these conflicts are officially over, the aftermath can last for decades, so deep is the devastation they have wrought. Cambodian education is still recovering from Pol Pot.

Children are among the main casualties of these conflicts. One in three children in conflict zones does not go to school, compared to one in eleven in comparable low-income countries. Thanks to the pursuit of the Millennium Development Goals the number of children out of school in the world fell by 40% to 72m in 2010. The fall in places affected by conflict has been just 14%. Half the more than 70m children out of school are now in conflict zones. About 18.5m children are displaced persons, fleeing conflict or natural disasters.

The education of these children, and therefore their future, is almost certain to be deeply blighted. Conflict exacerbates the huge problems they already face. The poorest children in Somalia get just 0.4 years of schooling; the wealthiest 6.6 years. In many of these countries education is free in name but in reality parents have to pay fees, even to go to state schools. In the Democratic Republic of the Congo, 80–90% of families outside the capital Kinshasa pay fees to go to government school. Girls are particularly vulnerable. In many countries parents will not send girls to a school with male teachers. Yet in South Sudan, for example, only 7% of teachers are women. In Angola, 10% of boys drop out of school in grade three, but 25% of girls drop out at the same stage.

In Southern Sudan

only 7%

of teachers are women.

School buildings are often casualties of war. Save the Children estimates that in Afghanistan 50% of school lessons take place in tents or the open air because so many schools have been destroyed. In Nepal schools became pawns in the conflict between the Maoist guerillas and the government. The guerillas would take over a village school as a base for several months, ejecting the teachers and children. When the army found the guerillas, the school would be destroyed to prevent them coming back. If conflict means there are fewer schools and children have to travel further, girls are the first to suffer. In Afghanistan schools that are within one mile of a village get a 70% enrolment rate; if the school is more than two miles away the enrolments fall to 30%. Most of the dropouts are girls. It is almost impossible to get trained teachers in conflict zones. In Afghanistan, Angola, Nepal and South Sudan less than half the teachers have been to secondary school. Between 20% and 50% of children at Grade 3 in these countries cannot read.

These places attracted Tove Wang, a short, blond Norwegian. After years of working for Save the Children she had grown frustrated that they were not making more impact. So, along with some colleagues Wang came up with a plan to make a real difference: to improve the education of 8m of the poorest, most vulnerable children in the world. Plenty of people thought she was mad. Everyone agreed change was needed. Save the Children had been running vital education programmes in conflict zones for years. Yet few thought these efforts could be scaled up rapidly. Conflict zones were too uncertain, complicated, fragile and insecure, they warned. Money could disappear into the coffers of warlords and corrupt governments. The greatest sceptics, she says, were the same people who doubted The Citizens Foundation: professional educationalists.

The campaign that Wang and her team devised – Rewrite the Future – was the first to involve all 29 national members of the Save the Children movement. At the outset there were just five people, working in Oslo and London. They set themselves an extraordinary goal: to significantly improve the education of 8m children, including getting 3m into school for the first time. They gave themselves five years. Wang was unapologetic: "We wanted a goal that would stretch us, not just business as usual. That would not make the kind of change we needed."

They campaigned to get donor governments, companies and aid agencies to focus on the plight of children in conflict zones. They pointed out that the Millennium Development Goals would be missed because children in conflict zones were not in school. Each year they named and shamed governments that were not fulfilling their aid pledges. They got the issue onto the agenda of the UN and the G8. "Initially we had credibility because of the work we did on the ground. But then the campaign gained its own momentum and we constantly fed it with new issues," Wang explained. The five core team members

Pupils in a maths lesson
at St Peter's Murambi School
(Kasese District), Uganda

"We wanted a goal that would stretch us, not just business as usual. That would not make the kind of change we needed."

TOP: Children from St Peter's Murambi school play on open ground above the school; **MIDDLE, LEFT TO RIGHT:** Figures showing rising enrolments at Kiburara School; A welcome sign at Kiburara School; Children in a fishing village on the edge of Lake George; **BOTTOM:** Teacher at Kiburara School

organised countless committees, stakeholder groups and mini-campaigns, which in turn involved thousands of other people. It became a movement. They raised an additional $450m to invest in education in zones of conflict.

That was probably the easy part. The hard part was investing that money in 20 of the most difficult countries in the world and in a way that could be monitored and evaluated to show the donors it was working. Wang's plans met with widespread doubt even from within Save the Children. It took her a year to persuade Save the Children teams in these countries that they could build the hundreds of new schools needed.

No two conflicts are alike. So in each place they had to employ a slightly different approach. In Afghanistan they worked with local village councils, *shura*, to create education committees, which then found a local home or mosque in which classes could be led by a trusted local teacher. Much of the work in Afghanistan went into expanding informal education, outside school. In South Sudan, after the peace agreement was signed, they trained thousands of teachers to work in former war zones. In Côte d'Ivoire they established more than 100 children's clubs to give them a voice in education policy. In Uganda, and many other places, they introduced accelerated learning programmes so that older children who had missed out on primary school could get seven years education compressed into just three. In northern Uganda, for example, more than 800 young mothers, aged 12–20, completed their primary school education on an accelerated learning programme. In Afghanistan 450 accelerated learning centres were built. In Sudan more than 3,500 former child soldiers went through an accelerated programme. Save the Children did very little of this work themselves. Mostly they worked with local partners, mainly NGOs, to deliver. Only in places such as Darfur where there were no NGOs did Save the Children step in itself.

Wang and her team missed their goal. Creating schools from scratch, even informal learning centres, proved more difficult than they had anticipated. Even so they managed to get 1.6m children into school for the first time: that is 876 children enrolled in school for the first time, every day for five years. Save the Children has committed to meeting the 3m target by 2015. They failed to hit their other target too: they did not improve the education of 8m children, as planned, but instead reached 10m. They did that by building or improving two schools a day, every day, for five years. In some places the campaign itself changed the conflict. In Nepal they got the government and the guerillas to take schools out of the conflict. The campaign also supported more than 4,000 children's clubs that provide children with a permanent voice in education policy. In Liberia and Sierra Leone, education has become one of the top priorities for the new governments ushered into power after the conflict.

Reflecting back on the five years in which she and four other people set out to change the world, Wang, modest and unassuming, smiles lightly: "We did not realize how much power we had. Really we should have aimed higher. The bolder you are, the more doors open to you. We've only just scratched the surface." In the Democratic Republic of the Congo alone 166,000 teachers would be needed to make primary education universal. The Central African Republic would need to increase the number of teachers by 18.5% a year for the foreseeable future to meet that goal.

Yet the biggest lesson from the Rewrite the Future campaign is that getting children into school is not enough on its own. In too many places Wang's team built better schools but there were not enough properly trained teachers. In other places children went to school for the first time only to be subjected to hours of rote learning mandated by a distant Ministry of Education. This is how Tove Wang summed it up: "Really we needed to focus on learning and outcomes rather than school. Good teachers are more important for learning than good buildings."

Wang's conclusions are borne out by our other innovators. Many of them, like Rewrite the Future, focus on getting more children into school: we call these "who" innovations because their main focus is on removing barriers to **who** gets education. These innovations are the focus of the next chapter. Yet innovations that just focus on expanding access to school are unlikely to be enough to improve outcomes. What also matters is **how** children learn, what they learn and whether they feel motivated to do so. That is why our innovators often combine measures to increase access with changes in how traditional educational models operate. Those are: **how** innovations which change how people learn; **why** innovations which focus on motivating children to learn in new ways and **what** innovations which focus on the content, skills and knowledge that people acquire when they are learning. Our innovators open up access to education but they also change it, by creating different, better, more effective and rewarding ways for children to learn. Let's start with the first of those tasks, opening up access to learning.

In northern Uganda, for example, more than

800

young mothers, aged 12–20, completed their primary school education on an accelerated learning programme.

A message at Kibwrara School,
Kasese District, Uganda

WHO: OVERCOMING BARRIERS TO ACCESS

Children in a village affected
by civil conflict in Uganda,
which has benefited
from investment by Rewrite
the Future

It is a daily routine in hundreds of millions of homes. Parents give their children breakfast, make sure they are properly dressed and check they have what they need for school: books, homework, pencils, rulers, perhaps some gym kit. Then they dispatch them to school in good faith that for the next few hours, with their friends, they will learn and have fun, to return home, tired but happy, with their minds just a little more open to the world.

That is the way it is meant to be. But for many millions of children, due to a variety of obstacles, school is difficult to get to. School might be too far away. Their parents might not want them to go. They may need to stay at home to work or to look after their siblings. Many children do not have average needs, nor do they live in average places. Getting these children to school requires doing things differently and sometimes that means seeing that people can access education without having to go to a school.

The innovations with the greatest potential to open up access to learning involve communication technologies that can

ABOVE: A student heads into class at the Massachusetts Institute of Technology, Boston; **RIGHT:** MIT, which launched the OpenCourse-Ware programme in 2002 to promote the spread of knowledge

make learning possible without a student having to be in the same room as a teacher. The most significant innovation in this field is the open courseware movement that started at the Massachusetts Institute of Technology in 2001.

Gilbert Strang is an unlikely rock star. Middle-aged, mild-mannered, Strang's creative work is done in a room overflowing with papers and books. Yet his YouTube channel has had millions of hits. More than 3.75m people have downloaded his work. Strang is a rock star in the field of algebra.

Strang has taught mathematics at university for most of his adult life, much of that time at MIT, with relatively small classes. When in 2001 MIT decided it would make its courses – lectures, lecture notes, reading lists, exam questions – available for free online, Strang's course, 18.06 Linear Algebra, was one of the first in line. Since then it has had 2.25m visits and the YouTube channel accompanying the course has had 1.3m views. It is the most used algebra course in human history.

The story of how Strang came to acquire his worldwide following amongst algebra fans started at the height of the dot. com boom of the late 1990s. MIT's senior staff were concerned it was losing ground to the likes of Columbia and Yale, which were busy creating businesses to exploit the Internet's educational potential. MIT wanted to make its mark but was not quite sure how. A committee of academics explored the business opportunities from every angle and came to the conclusion that many others would subsequently reach: it would be extremely difficult to make money on the web. The committee was about to throw in the towel when one of the academics said something that was both blindingly obvious yet deeply unconventional: "If we can't make money from our content, why don't we just give it away?"

That strategy had a major attraction: it was in line with MIT's purpose to develop open source technologies and software that can be used by anyone. Free, online access to its courses would further the institution's goal, to advance and spread knowledge wherever possible. There were some issues to get sorted before they could get going. Cecilia d'Oliveira, the technical director of the project, recalls it took about six months to get all the faculty on board. She made sure it would be painless for the teachers to create content; a special team was employed to record lessons and put the material online. The money was raised from the Hewlett Foundation, which has become the main global funder of the open educational resources movement. The site needed an intellectual property framework, which eventually came from adopting a Creative Commons license. They started in 2002 with 50 pilot courses, among them 18.06 Linear Algebra. Everything seemed to be going to plan. How wrong that plan was.

The business plan forecast that the site's main visitors would be educators using the content to enhance their courses. One teacher using a course might reach hundreds of students. Educators do use the site and 46% of those re-use the content in their own lessons. In Indonesia, to cite just one example, an entire university engineering curriculum has been based on MIT's material. Yet teachers make up only about 10% of the site's traffic. Most of the users are students and half of those are independent learners not affiliated to any institution. They are just people keen to learn. No one saw them coming. Much of that growth is due to a technology few foresaw back in the year 2000: the explosion of video on the Internet, through services such as YouTube and Vimeo. As Gilbert Strang puts it: "The video lecture is going to become the basic building block of post-secondary education in the future, much as the textbook is now."

The results are little short of staggering. By April 2011, the tenth anniversary of the decision to create the platform, there were 2,000 courses, drawing on contributions from 4,000 staff, from 33 academic fields, in all five MIT schools, and those materials had been visited more than 100m times by 72m unique visitors. Each month there are 1m visits to the MIT site and another 1m to other sites around the world that carry its content. MIT's pioneering innovation has inspired a movement of emulators.

In 2005 ten institutions came together in the first open courseware conference. By 2011 the OpenCourseWare Consortium comprised 80 universities and 130 other educational institutions from more than 45 countries. More than 250 sites around the world are copies of the main MIT site. The Turkish Ministry of Education has invested $1m in its open courseware programme. Japanese universities have developed sophisticated search tools so users can find just the right content. Vietnam and China, Taiwan and Korea, France and Spain have open courseware programmes. What Shigeru Miyagawa, MIT's director, calls a "collective act of intellectual philanthropy" is changing lives in millions of small ways.

Cecilia d'Oliveira has only just got started. "We are committed to having an even more dramatic impact in the decade to come," she says. Having reached 100m in the first decade she wants to reach 1bn in the decade to come. In the first ten years they helped 1m educators; in the next ten years they want to help 10m. She hopes to build stronger communities around the courses. A pilot with OpenStudy, a specialist in educational social networks, has helped create a community of 1,600 members around course 6.00 Introduction to Computer Science. Course 18.01 Single Variable Calculus has 1,400 members. Gilbert Strang is working on the equivalent of a new album, which promises to be an even bigger hit than Linear Algebra. His new project – Highlights of Calculus – is designed to make calculus accessible to a broader audience.

The real power of MIT's innovation is that it has created a model that others could follow. We are just at the very outset of exploring how the unfolding potential of social media and the World Wide Web can widen access to education and deepen the experience of learning. We will need a multitude of overlapping experiments, some free and some commercial, in many different settings, to show how students can access content more easily but also work on it together, add to it and share it.

One such experiment is taking place in Amazonas, the largest state in Brazil, an area of 1.5m square kilometres, where children in search of a decent secondary education usually have to move to the regional capital Manaus, which accounts for half of the 3.3m inhabitants. Many among the rural population come from one of 65 ethnic groups, each with a distinct culture and language. The Distance Learning in the Amazon project, sponsored by the Secretariat of Education and Hughes, the satellite company, delivers classes in real time. The classes are delivered from three studios in Manaus to 25,000 students, in 700 classrooms, in 300 schools scattered across the interior. By allowing students to attend local schools dropout rates are reduced. The contributions from specialist teachers in Manaus are complemented by 900 generalist teachers in the schools

More than

250 sites

around the world
are copies of
the main MIT site.

Professor Tito Okumu, the head of the physics department at Kampala University, one of many in the developing world to make use of MIT's OpenCourseWare platform

who have been trained to use the digital content to stimulate class discussion. Secondary pass rates have risen from 60% to 77% thanks to the project and the dropout rate reduced from 27% to 16%.

Research by the British Open University's Digital Education Enhancement Project in South Africa and Egypt found that people who lacked the traditional education systems were far more open to using new technologies for learning than their counterparts in the developed world. Yet in many of the poorest places reliable electricity and clean water are more of a priority than broadband and wi-fi. Remote places that lack schools are also not on the Internet. In much of Africa, even when Internet access is technically possible, it is prohibitively expensive. That is why it will be important to look at other combinations of technologies to bring learning to people.

The most obvious tools are smartphones, equipped with keypads, colour screens and, potentially, access to a myriad of apps. One glimpse of what is possible is provided by the Mobile Immersive Learning for Literacy in Emerging Economies project (MILLEE) which has created games to allow children living in slums to learn a "world" language in places and times that are more convenient than going to school. MILLEE started in India and early efforts are underway to replicate it in China (teaching both Mandarin and English), and in Kenya and Tanzania (teaching English). Bridges to the Future, a project started by Professor Dan Wagner, from the International Literacy

ABOVE: Pupils at the Juvvalapalem village primary school in West Godavari district, India, using IBM KidSmart computers to play Bridges to the Future's Telugu language software through Byrraju Foundation's Model School programme; **RIGHT:** Pupils at the Kallakuru village primary school in West Godavari district, India, playing the Bridges to the Future programme

"If we can't make money from our content, why don't we just give it away?"

Institute at the University of Pennsylvania, has taken a different approach, developing software for literacy programmes in native, minority languages to be used in schools in Andhra Pradesh in India and Limpopo in South Africa.

Older technologies, including books and pamphlets that can be used over and again by many people, remain among the most cost-effective ways to distribute content. Another is radio, which is still expanding its reach, especially in Africa, a century after it was first operational there. The Smallholders Farmers Rural Radio network in Nigeria, for example, brings useful information, knowledge and skills to hundreds of small-scale farmers, in isolated villages.

Technology alone cannot create an open education system. In many of the poorest, harshest places to reach, computer hardware is difficult to come by and too expensive to use. Computers are lifeless without software that makes them easy and interesting to engage with. Yet the lesson of MIT's experiment is that technology can change the rules of the game, tilting them in favour of people who want to learn, by making possible mass access at much lower cost than by traditional means. As Cecilia d'Oliveira puts it: "Human potential is universal, opportunity is not. The hundreds of thousands that visit our site each month are testament to the worldwide desire to learn and to the limited capacity of educational systems around the world to fulfill that desire."

One of the most promising initiatives to explore that potential is the Hole in the Wall programme launched by Indian educationalist Sugata Mitra.

Mitra put a computer in a hole in the external wall of his office in Hyderabad to see what the children living in the nearby slum would make of it. Within a few hours they had taught themselves to surf the Internet. Within a few weeks they were learning maths and English as well as searching for information. That experiment gave birth to one of the most radical educational innovations of our times, and one of the places where this revolution got started was the Madangir Resettlement Colony, a dense and dusty slum on the outskirts of New Delhi.

> "Human potential is universal, opportunity is not. The hundreds of thousands that visit our site each month are testament to the worldwide desire to learn."

Madangir has a new primary school and on paper the school does not seem too bad: the 320 pupils have 11 teachers. Yet all is not as it seems. The school is meant to teach in English but the headteacher speaks only Hindi. Madangir is typical of many Indian primary schools: often there are more than 50 pupils in a class because many teachers are absent and too many of those present are not teaching. Children sit in rows, looking bored, copying from the blackboard, parroting their teachers, too often barely seeming to understand what they are being taught.

Madangir was one of the places where Mitra began to explore how children could use computers to learn by themselves, and from one another, with minimal supervision. The computers, encased in heavy yellow metal, were specially adapted to withstand the dust, heat and thousands upon thousands of little fingers, pointing and pressing. The young people in the colony flocked to computers before and after school, where in eager groups they would go over and over the simple programmes that taught them maths, history and science. Since then Mitra has conducted scores of experiments to show how far children can go, with and without support, in and out of school, to use computers to learn. When he took computers to a remote rural area renowned for its singing, the children, who had never seen a computer before, needed just 24 hours to start recording songs. In a fishing village he showed that children could teach themselves the basics of biotechnology, in English, without the help of teachers. Elsewhere he has experimented with self-organised learning environments that sit half inside the school, the other half facing the street. In another iteration he has recruited retired teachers in England to teach students in India using Skype as a bridge. More than 500 computers have been installed in scores of sites in India and Africa, used by perhaps 1m children, especially in places where teachers are hard to find. Mitra does not believe technology should substitute for good teachers, but in places where it is difficult to recruit good teachers it could provide an alternative and scaleable way for children to learn without schools, classrooms and textbooks.

"Within a few hours they had taught themselves to surf the Internet [...]"

Children in schools in the West Godavari district who also use Bridges to the Future software programme to develop literacy in their native language, Telugu

ABOVE AND RIGHT: Children taking part in the Shine literacy programme at the Observatory school in Cape Town

Distance is just one obstacle to universal access to education. The most basic obstacle is poverty. Children from the very poorest backgrounds often cannot afford to go to school. In many countries secondary schools are free in name but not in practice. Parents are expected to pay for books, equipment, uniforms and food. The poorest families often cannot afford to forego the earnings of older children. That is why innovations such as Espacios para Crecer are important. Created in 2004, with the help of funding from the United States, Espacios para Crecer eliminates the worst forms of child labour in the Dominican Republic. More than 12,500 children between the ages of 6 and 13 have been through its informal education programmes that gradually wean children away from work and into school.

Health is another huge issue. The 2010 Education for All Global Monitoring Report estimated than 175m children a year enter primary school having suffered malnutrition at some point. Globally about 272m school days a year are lost to diarrhoea, and around 400m school-age children are infected with worms that cause anaemia. In Nepal, Save the Children dewormed 300,000 children, which enabled many to attend school more regularly and learn more.

Language and culture pose other barriers. The chance to learn a world language – English or Spanish for example – is part of what attracts people to formal education. Yet the standardisation of curriculum around these languages can also exclude people, especially recent immigrants and minority groups. That is why innovators are devising ways to overcome language as a barrier to access. Gateway to the Future is a programme devised in New Jersey in the United States, which allows Hispanic students to gain credits by completing their first-year courses at college in Spanish, giving them time to build up their English skills. The bilingual first-year programme markedly reduces dropouts among Hispanic students who often fail their exams, not because their content knowledge is limited, but because of their poor English.

In Burkina Faso the exclusive use of French as the main medium of instruction is one factor to blame for high dropout rates. Of 1,000 children entering primary school only 205 reach grade six without repeating a year and the average pass rate for the school leaving certificate is 40%. To address those shortcomings the Bilingual Education Continuum has created 27 community pre-school education spaces and 119 bilingual primary schools so that children can learn in one of the five national languages as well as French. Not only have pass rates risen but many children complete primary school in five rather than six years. Pass rates are 89% compared with 69% in French-speaking schools. In 2010 the Ministry of Education announced plans to transform 21 classical schools into bilingual schools and to build 100 new ones.

Children in South Africa, brought up in Khosa-speaking homes, face a huge challenge in Year 5: they have to start learning in English. The vocabulary they are expected to master more than doubles. Not surprisingly those with little preparation quickly fall behind and are the most likely to drop out. Maurita Weisenberg set up the Shine project to stem that flow of dropouts. Thanks to sponsorship from local companies, Shine provides volunteer readers in six Cape Town schools, who spend two hours a week, for 32 weeks, reading one-on-one with children in Year 2. Shine assesses 1,000 children a year across the six schools and targets its effort on the 350 who are most at risk of falling behind in Year 3. Once behind, these children rarely catch up. Teachers, who have had little more than secondary education themselves, often lack the time and the skills to give these children the attention they need. With the help of Shine's volunteers at the Observatory School, close to downtown Cape Town, the success rate in reading tests at Year 3 rose from 50% to more than 80%. Weisenberg explains: "If we can make just a small investment in them at this stage, to help them get over the hump, then it can pay dividends later. The truth is that with a bit of attention, you breathe on these kids and off they go."

Children in distinct tribal and ethnic groups face particular disadvantages. In India the literacy rate among tribal populations in rural areas such as Orissa state is as low as 29%. The Kalinga Institute of Social Sciences started life in 1993 with 125 students from a tribal slum in Bhubaneswar. In 2011 it got 50,000 applications and educated more than 10,000 children a year from 62 tribes, in a residential school that mixes formal and vocational training in computing, electronics, tailoring and food processing. Children are encouraged to earn while they learn, making products to be sold in the market. The dropout rate is 0%.

Sadly conflict and distance, poverty and language do not exhaust the obstacles children face in accessing a decent education. Two of the most intractable are disability and gender.

Of 1,000 children entering primary school only 205 reach grade six without repeating a year and the average pass rate for the school leaving certificate is

40%.

"We want to help families to understand that having a disabled child is not an affliction or something to be ashamed of, to be shy about."

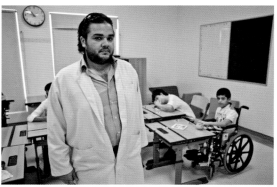

ABOVE AND RIGHT: Staff at the Shaffalah Center, Doha, Qatar

Disability compounds all the other factors that disadvantage children. According to the World Health Organization about 150m children up to the age of 14 live with a disability. Children with a disability are far less likely to make it to school in the first place and to complete their studies. A WHO survey in 51 countries, between 2002 and 2004, found that 61% of boys completed their primary education, but only 50% of disabled boys. In low income countries only 45% of disabled boys and 32% of disabled girls completed their primary education. Children with disability face significant disadvantages, even in the richest countries. In the United States only 10% of young people with a disability make it to college. In much of the world young people with disabilities face even grimmer prospects: shut away and shunned by families that are ashamed of them.

Yet innovation often comes from outside the mainstream and so it has proved with the education of disabled children. New models of education have been developed to help the disabled which involve personalised learning, intensive work with families at home and holistic approaches that bring together academic, health and social professionals.

The Shafallah Center started life in the late 1990s with just 40 disabled students in a few houses in Doha, Qatar. By 2011 it catered for 600 disabled students, about 75 of them with autism, in a state of the art campus, with seven school units in 18 connected buildings and with almost 600 staff. Shafallah is a school, but one which works only by departing from the standard models.

Shafallah starts work with the families of disabled children soon after they are born. Hassan Ali Bin Ali, the chairman and driving force behind the centre, explained: "We are very family-focused. We want to help families to understand that having a disabled child is not an affliction or something to be ashamed of, to be shy about." When children are enrolled, Shafallah's multidisciplinary team take a month to assess their needs. Each student gets an individualised learning programme. The light and airy classrooms are designed for classes of no more than eight students. Each chair and table has been designed to adjust to the person using it. The corridors and doors in all the buildings are wide enough to take a car.

Hassan's team created the centre by drawing on the best ideas from around the world. The Shafallah swimming pool, which is used intensively for hydrotherapy, is based on technology from Sweden. The slatted floor rises to allow wheelchairs to be wheeled onto it. It is lowered into the water to just the right depth for the children in that class. Staff were recruited from all over the Middle East: speech therapists from Tunisia, special needs teachers from Jordan. A world-class centre for genetic research is attached to the centre, which is staffed by scientists from around the world working with state of the art equipment. Their research is shared with more than 20 leading universities, as well as helping parents to understand what might be in store for their children.

Whatever the obstacles a child faces in accessing education – poverty, language, distance, conflict, disability – all are made more daunting if the child is a girl. Girls make up 57% of those not allowed to attend primary school. If girls' participation in education matched that of boys around the world 3.6m more girls would be in school. In developing countries, according to UNICEF, one in five girls makes it to primary school but does not complete their education. No African country sends more than half its girls to secondary school. In South Sudan girls aged 15 are more likely to die in childbirth than to complete primary school.

More girls are going to school but even now too many are not finishing school. That inequality is all the more troubling because educating girls delivers huge social payoffs. Once women gain a basic education they are likely to have fewer children and more likely to invest in their education. Women who can read instructions on medicines and water-purifying equipment are better able to look after their children. Women with education are more able to work, less dependent upon men and so less exposed to sexual violence and HIV. Yet despite the clear benefits of educating more women, two thirds of the world's 760m illiterate adults are women.

Many of our innovators are working on ways to minimise the disadvantages suffered by girls. The Citizens Foundation employs only women teachers to make parents feel more secure in sending their daughters to school. Families are often loath to lose the income that girls earn. That is why Rewrite the Future worked with families in Sudan to make sure they made up the income they lost by sending girls to school. Technology may play a role: MILLEE's mobile phone learning games are designed so that girls who are not at school can learn in the downtime between their chores. One of the most impressive initiatives, Nanhi Kali in India, is one of the simplest.

ABOVE: Pupil in Elurupadu village primary school in West Godavari district, India; **RIGHT:** Girl with bananas outside Kallakuru village primary school in West Godavari district, India

"Whatever the obstacles a child faces in accessing education –poverty, language, distance, conflict, disability– all are made more daunting if the child is a girl."

Down a muddy lane near the North Joshi Marg in Mumbai, a little girl sits under some tarpaulin doing her homework. This is Nasreen Ansari's home: a tent with mud sloshing around it from the monsoon rains. Nasreen is the youngest of five children. Her illiterate mother is a domestic cleaner; her father a jobbing construction labourer. They came to the city looking for a better future. Nasreen could be it. She is the first girl in her family to go to school. Quiet but steely and sharp, she is determined to succeed.

Like many girls of her age, Nasreen starts her day at 6am by getting water and preparing the family breakfast. Once that is cleared away she's off to school as early as possible. Nasreen's determination has been reinforced by a simple but highly effective support network for girls from poor backgrounds who attend public schools. Nanhi Kali, which means "the girl child", has given Nasreen the uniform and bag she is so proud of. When she started school she looked like a street urchin. Now she makes sure she looks neat and smart. Each day, along with the other Nanhi Kali girls in her school, Nasreen gets an extra hour with a support worker to reinforce the basics of reading, writing and maths.

In 1996 Nanhi Kali reached 1,700 girls with a fairly haphazard programme. By 2011 it was supporting

70,000 girls

Sheetal Mheta, the poised and youthful driving force behind Nanhi Kali, explains what girls in India are up against: "In India girls are looked upon as liabilities; sons are looked upon as assets. Very often parents are not willing to invest in their education because they expect the girls are going to get married off into another family. So there is no point in investing in that girl's education." Government schools, free in name, come with significant costs: parents have to buy uniforms and school books. Parents grow quickly unwilling to shoulder those costs if girls come home from poorly run schools without having learned anything. In those circumstances parents are likely to want girls to be useful, to make a contribution to household tasks. "Girls aged five, six, seven – they all know how to cook," remarks Mheta.

The idea to support girls in the face of these pressures came from the business leader Anand Gopal Mahindra in 1996. Mheta was employed to channel funds from the K.C. Mahindra Educational Trust to NGOs working with girls. The scheme took off in 2005 when Mahindra allied with the Naandi Foundation, which was already working with thousands of children through its Ensuring Children Learn programme. The Mahindra Educational Trust fundraises for the programme, mainly by tapping large corporations, while Naandi runs the educational programmes.

Nanhi Kali is disarmingly simple but highly effective. Full-time academic resource coodinators work with four or five schools to train "community activists" who run the sessions with the girls. The "community activists" act as para-teachers and mentors for the children, liaising with the school and their parents. At Nasreen's school the "community activist" intervened to stop a girl's alcoholic father taking her out of school to sell her into domestic service. The hour-long classes after school help to reinforce what the girls have learned at school. "If you can get them to master the basics, that can go a long way," Mheta explained. "They are less likely to fall behind then." Initially Naandi's classes followed a fairly traditional format, the girls seated in rows with the "community activist" teacher at the front. More recently, after examining what approaches worked best, Naandi introduced what it describes as a more reflexive and collaborative model, in which girls sit in circles and help one another.

In 1996 Nanhi Kali reached 1,700 girls with a fairly haphazard programme. By 2011 it was supporting 70,000 girls, half of them in rural and tribal areas in eight Indian states, with a structured programme that is systematically funded by contributions from companies.

The girls say they like the informal atmosphere, the special activities that Nanhi Kali lays on, and especially the smart uniform. Their mothers say Nanhi Kali gives for free what richer parents have to pay for: extra tuition to make sure girls do not drown in the mediocrity of the government school system. All the mothers we talked to at Nasreen's school said they wanted their daughters to carry on studying before they got married, so that they had a measure of economic independence. All over India millions of mothers are seeing in their daughters a future they could have only dreamed of.

When Nasreen's father was asked what he hopes for her future, he shrugged and replied: "It is up to her." That idea in itself is a mini-revolution.

ABOVE, FROM BOTTOM TO TOP: Nasreen with her father and neighbours; walking through the slum; cows at rest in the street

RIGHT, MAIN IMAGE: Nasreen Ansari outside her school, just down the road from her home in Lower Parel, Mumbai

Far too many children are cut off from a decent education by conflict and poverty, distance and geography, language and culture, disability and gender. For children who often face a combination of these obstacles, standard schools that follow the standard model may well not be the solution. Overcoming these obstacles requires innovation: accelerated and vocational learning; different kinds of schools, in different buildings; more informal out of school support programmes; technologies that allow learning in remote places; women teachers who make parents feel safe sending girls to school. Getting more children into school in itself requires a mass of ingenuity to overcome the very different obstacles they face. But as Tove Wang of the Rewrite the Future campaign found, that will not be enough to improve outcomes. In too many schools teachers who are poorly trained and paid, under-managed and under-motivated, follow a rigid and academic curriculum to deliver formulaic and unengaging lessons to children seated in rows, who copy and chant. If they learn anything, they do so by rote, without understanding the meaning of what they learn. Too many children are not at school. But too many are at schools where they learn too little. To change that requires something more than wider access, it means innovating new and more effective ways for children to learn.

BELOW: Children outside their classroom at Kallakuru village primary school in West Godavari district, India; **BELOW LEFT:** Girl outside Gollalakoderu village primary school, West Godavari district, India; **RIGHT:** Slum neighbourhood in Poddaer Mills, Dilai Road, Sohrab Chawl, Mumbai, home to many families with daughters enrolled in the Nanhi Kali programme

Classroom in Bhimavaram,
India

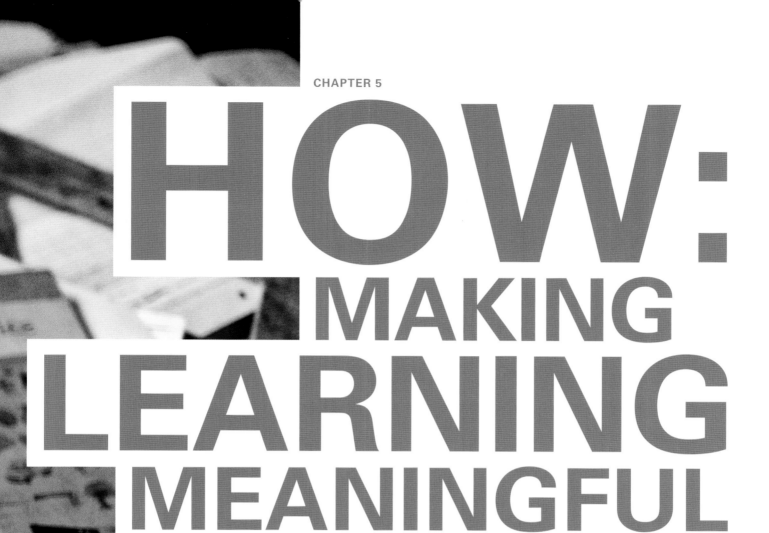

CHAPTER 5

HOW: MAKING LEARNING MEANINGFUL

The traditional tools
of teaching, Uganda

Too many children go to school believing it to be a gateway to opportunity, only to find themselves sat in rows, learning by rote, bored out of their minds, physically present but psychologically absent. This traditional model of learning by instruction and repetition, drilled by a teacher standing at the front of the class, might be a good way to memorise multiplication tables but it is hugely ineffective in all other respects. Children who have learned to give the right responses when asked a question may not understand the underlying principles of what they are learning. They can parrot answers without understanding what they mean. They can come up with the right answer when they are familiar with the question but not understand how to apply their knowledge in new ways, in different settings. All too easily children can become bored, demotivated. For some, the material will be impenetrable. Others will find it dull and too easy. If a hard-pressed or inflexible teacher cannot provide these children with the attention they need they will become disengaged and some will drift away. Even if children do manage to stay engaged, this approach is hugely ineffective in encouraging children to explore interesting questions together, to share ideas and to learn how to apply the knowledge they have in new situations. Yet this is still the dominant way that classrooms are set up and lessons delivered. Extensive reviews of teaching in Kenya, Ghana, Uganda, Malawi and several other African states concluded that the dominant mode of teaching remains a teacher-led transmission style in which pupil talk is restricted to short, often chorused answers to closed questions.

These rigid, inflexible and often unproductive approaches to learning partly explain why increased investments in school have not delivered improved results, especially for children from poorer backgrounds. Investing more in ineffective teaching will not deliver better results. As Linda Darling-Hammond shows in *The Flat World and Education*, many of the same trends are at work in US schooling. Extra investment in ineffective teaching is unlikely to have an impact on outcomes. More investment is needed but in different, better and more effective approaches to learning.

Our pioneers get more children into education but many also change how students learn once they are in school. In this section we focus on three initiatives that face quite different challenges, but which deploy similar approaches to make learning highly engaging.

Most schools are still
organised as this one
is in Uganda, with
children seated in rows,
listening to a teacher,
learning by rote
and chanting answers

Training teachers so they have the confidence and skills to prepare and facilitate more exciting, challenging and interesting lessons is vital to creating experiences that engage students. It is a challenge all over the world, but particularly in Africa.

"Teachers trained through TESSA are: hosting richer and more open question and answer session with their pupils; employing teaching methods that involve more problem-solving."

Ghana has only a quarter of the teachers it needs to provide universal primary education and Lesotho only a fifth. UNICEF estimates 1m children lose their teachers each year to HIV/AIDS. In Sub-Saharan Africa half of primary school teachers have few, or no, qualifications at all. In Tanzania one estimate is that only 230 primary school teachers have a higher education qualification. The expansion of African education systems has exacerbated issues of quality: in Nigeria between 1999 and 2002, as enrolments in primary school went up, so the proportion of qualified teachers fell from 97% to 72%. These less-qualified teachers will confront very large, demanding classes. In Western Kenya it's commonplace for teachers to be responsible for classes of 80 pupils. The answer to these challenges, however, may not lie in traditional approaches to teacher training, which in Africa is heavy on theory and light on practice. Trained teachers have few peers to look to for models of innovative practice. Most will have been to highly traditional schools. They will have extremely limited opportunities for in-service training. In these conditions how is it possible to promote more imaginative and creative approaches to learning?

It was to address these challenges that the British Open University, working with universities and teacher training institutions in 12 African countries, created the Teacher Education in Sub-Saharan Africa (TESSA) online network in 1995.

ABOVE: Emmanuel Kambale (right) at Kinyateke School, Kasese District, Uganda; **RIGHT:** Emmanuel Kambale at his desk

Freda Wolfenden, TESSA's director, puts the challenge and the opportunity this way: "If we are to meet the scale of need for teacher education and training over the coming decades then we must accept that the bricks and mortar institutions, built to train teachers in the twentieth century, will be wholly insufficient to meet need in the twenty-first century." As the demand for more, better-trained teachers becomes more acute so will the need for creative, low cost responses.

TESSA is based on the Open University's tried and tested modules for training British teachers already at work in schools. That content has been rewritten by more than 700 African educators to fit with the teacher training and curriculum requirements in Nigeria, Sudan, Kenya, South Africa, Rwanda, Ghana, Zambia, Uganda and Tanzania. The result is a large online bank of open access educational resources that teachers can turn to for ideas to make lessons more interesting, from investigating electricity to understanding poetry. The 75 modules, in 12 languages, provided by the 18 partner institutions in Africa, are used to train between 300,000 and 400,000 teachers a year. In Nigeria the National Teacher's Institute has incorporated several modules in courses for tens of thousands of teachers. In Ghana and Rwanda the modules are used by hundreds of teachers, to pursue their own in-service training. Countries that are not part of the official TESSA network – Mauritius and Togo – are also using the platform.

TESSA's aim is not just to provide more training, but to change what happens in classrooms by inspiring teachers to adopt more imaginative ways to teach. "We cannot change the curriculum in these countries," Wolfenden explains. "But we can gradually have an impact, culturally, on teaching methods." TESSA is giving teachers the confidence and tools to go against the grain, to prepare more exciting, engaging and challenging lessons. Teacher by teacher, lesson by lesson, evaluations show that teachers trained through TESSA are: hosting richer and more open question and answer session with their pupils; employing teaching methods that involve more problem-solving; getting out of the classroom to use the immediate environment of the school to stimulate learning; encouraging group work, dialogue and games alongside traditional whole-class teaching. As one evaluation from Egerton University in Kenya remarked: teachers even report finding their jobs interesting and exciting.

Thousands of miles away the same principles are being applied in rural and city schools in Latin America.

Marina Castro cheerfully admits she did not have a clue what she was doing when she started her career as a teacher in a small rural school in Colombia. She was on her own, trying to teach about 50 children of all ages. It was not the idyllic world of the wicker fence and single-room schoolhouse of _Little House on the Prairie:_ "Nothing had prepared me for it. I had no tools to handle a multi-grade school. After a couple of weeks I was on the verge of giving up." Then she struck lucky. A colleague introduced her to a three-week training course in a teaching method designed to help teachers like her. Escuela Nueva is a way for teachers to get pupils into groups for self-organised learning using step-by-step learning guides. When these guides arrived in Uganda they became known as "silent teachers."

Colombia has been pursuing universal primary education since the 1950s. By 1994 eight out of ten children were enrolled, but in reality access was highly unequal: 89% of city children were in school against only 66% in rural areas. Eight out of ten rural primary age children were in multi-grade schools like Marina Castro's. If all students are not fully occupied then their time on task falls, their achievement drops and they can quickly get bored: discipline degenerates, the teacher feels they are losing control and they become frustrated and feel overworked. Not surprisingly, multi-grade schools with traditional teaching methods deliver poor results: in the 1980s only 59% of first-grade students in these primary schools progressed to second grade, compared with 74% in urban schools.

Vicky Colbert, the founder of Escuela Nueva, came at the problems of multi-grade schools from an unusual angle. She had been educated at the American school in Bogotá and then Stanford University, in California. When she returned to Colombia, to work in the Ministry of Education, she chose not to work in the heart of the system, nor in a rich urban school, but at the margins, with the poorest, worst-performing multi-grade schools because they were most in need of innovation. Colbert picked up the model of unitary schools, promoted by UNESCO in the 1960s, which encouraged a degree of structured self-instruction. She combined that with ideas she had returned with from her studies, inspired by Dewey and Montessori. She worked with rural educators who were already instinctively putting into practice similar ideas. Escuela Nueva developed over several years through this interaction between philosophy and practice. The method is almost Socratic, posing children questions and challenging them to justify their answers. If several

groups can be encouraged to learn this way then the teacher can devote more time to other children who need more help.

That is not the only benefit. In a traditional school children who miss a term, for example to work on the family farm, would have to repeat an entire year. In an Escuela Nueva school children are able to learn at their own pace, dipping in and out of school as their family's economic circumstances demand. Repetition and dropout rates are reduced. Escuela Nueva schools are more likely to engage local communities, research shows, and that means they are twice as likely as a public school to have a library.

"The danger in education is that responses to failure tend to be administrative – changing how systems work, centralising or decentralising, new reporting systems," Colbert says. "The key is to change how learning takes place, which means new approaches to pedagogy. The teacher has to become a facilitator, to motivate the children to learn rather than transmit knowledge to them."

It does not take long to train a teacher in the Escuela Nueva model: they have three weeks of training spread across a year, followed up by regular bouts of in-service training. When that training is done well it can have a lasting impact, as Marina Castro explained: "The beauty of this approach is that the teacher does not have to know everything to be able to teach the children. In Escuela Nueva, the teacher facilitates more, and can focus more on their relationships with children rather than pushing information at them. It's a more horizontal, less vertical relationship. The children become more autonomous, develop their own talents and learn how to express themselves, to become protagonists. A teacher has to be trained to do it and they have to be consistent. It has to be a whole approach: you have to learn how to dance with the materials to make it work."

Escuela Nueva, working in the very poorest schools, has created a model of learning which is participative, collaborative and flexible. Children will not be sitting in rows in an Escuela Nueva school listening to a teacher, copying from the black-

Vicky Colbert, the founder of Escuela Neuva, in her office in Bogotá, Colombia

board, chanting the same answers together. They should be sitting in circles, in discussion, figuring out how best to work through the tasks set by the learning guide. Colbert says the children are learning not just maths and Spanish but the skills of negotiation and compromise, to be self-governing citizens, to live in a community together. Many of the places to which Escuela Nueva has spread have been ravaged by dictatorship, civil wars, guerrilla insurgency, drug cartels and paramilitaries operating above and beyond the law. In those places, schools that give children an experience of what it means to be self-governing citizens are huge innovations.

Escuela Nueva started in 1975 in 150 tiny rural schools. By 2011 it was operating in almost 17,000 Colombian schools and had been taken up in 19 countries, from Guatemala to Brazil. In that time its methods have been used with perhaps 5m children. Far fewer students drop out at Escuela Nueva schools. The system retains children of all abilities. Yet even so, pupils in Escuela Nueva schools outscore their counterparts in standard rural schools and Colombia is one of the few countries in the world where rural schools often perform better than urban schools.

Escuela Nueva is reaching middle age. The ideas it is based on are even older. Very few of the schools where it is employed have computers and the Internet. Many have no electricity much of the time. Yet Escuela Nueva is encouraging what many would describe as the most contemporary of twenty-first century skills: collaborative problem-solving and creativity.

Thousand of miles away and in very different conditions, working with very different students, many of the same principles are at work, in a remarkable project that started life in the sleepy surfers' resort of Muizenberg, near Cape Town, South Africa. One road back from shore, where surfers park their cars and come and go in wetsuits, a 1930s hotel has been transformed to become the home of an intense community of teachers and students drawn together by their shared passion for mathematical sciences.

The African Institute of Mathematical Sciences (AIMS) is the brainchild of the theoretical physicists Neil Turok and Fritz Hahne. Turok is the son of communists, prominent members of the African National Congress. Hahne's parents were German missionaries. Together they have created a strange hybrid. They are mathematical science missionaries. Like

their parents they want to build a pan-African movement. But their movement will not be made up of pastors and churches, hymns and sermons, and comrades in cells, but statisticians and physicists, epidemiologists and engineers, trained to tackle Africa's multiple challenges. Hahne and Turok have created a model educational community which aims to spawn an African mathematics movement.

Formally, AIMS is the product of a partnership between three South African universities – Cape Town, Stellenbosch and Western Cape – and the universities of Cambridge, Oxford and Paris-Sud, and it draws on faculty from universities around the world. But AIMS is no ordinary educational institution and, so long as Turok and Hahne have their way, it will never be part of a normal university because that would cramp its style.

AIMS recruits outstanding undergraduates from universities the length and breadth of Africa. Each is given a full scholarship worth about $10k a year. Komi Afassinou, a lithe, sparkling young mathematician from Togo who makes complex differential equations dance across the blackboard, is a typical recruit. One of 21 siblings, even if Afassinou had got the offer of a place at a university in South Africa or Europe he could never have afforded the air fare to take him to an interview. AIMS, however, pays for all of that. The 50 students, a third of whom are women, spend ten intense months living and working together on the Muizenberg campus. The student quarters are on the upper floors just above the seminar rooms. They eat all their meals in the light and friendly cafeteria. Every day everything

Students at **AIMS** learn mainly
through group discussions

Komi Afassinou, a young
mathematician from Togo
and AIMS student, whose
speciality is complex
differential equations

"It is so intense
because people live,
work and eat together
and they learn
an enormous
amount without
even realising it."

stops for afternoon tea in the lobby. Bruce Bassett works at AIMS' cosmology research centre located in some elegant, restored Italianate villas across the road from the hotel, where he researches the nature of dark matter. Bassett has watched several cohorts of students come and go: "Each year a new group of students come and yet each year the same sense of community emerges. It is so intense because people live, work and eat together and they learn an enormous amount without even realising it."

Many of the students are held back, not by their maths but their poor English; so a specialist language teacher is on hand. Most amazing, to many of them, the centre is equipped with a computer room connected to the Internet that is open all day, every day. For many it will be the first time they have used a computer for more than half an hour at a time and few of them will ever have used a computer to do maths. The students are

often brilliant but they have had an uneven education. If the university they went to happened to have the right books and a good teacher, they will have mastered the most complex of subjects. Often there will be huge gaps in their knowledge of basic mathematics simply because the university did not have the right books and teachers. They will have been taught in the most conventional ways, with a teacher at the front of the class, delivering a lecture, with little time for questions and no room for interaction. As Eve Lillian, who studied at the National University of Rwanda, put it: "The lecturers were the big guys, like God, you never got to talk to them."

AIMS turns all of that on its head with an approach designed to develop and round out the students, as people and as mathematicians, rather than imparting lumps of knowledge to them. In the first three months they study basic courses in topics such as mathematical problem-solving, modelling and computing.

In the next three months they focus on areas of special interest, such as Bayesian statistics, mathematical finance and non-linear waves. In the final stage they develop an extended essay, which involves extensive research and oral examination. In 2010 Juliet Nakakawa, from Uganda, who is now doing a master's at Stellenbosch University, wrote a paper on the risks of tuberculosis in old age; Paul Kibet Korir, from Kenya, who is now doing a PhD at the National University of Ireland, in Galway, wrote his dissertation on Epitope Discovery with Phylogenetic Hidden Markov Models. Each year about 25 international lecturers, drawn from a pool of 450 volunteers, come for three weeks at a time to teach informal courses that particularly interest them.

ABOVE: A student outside the centre at AIMS; **RIGHT:** Professor Fritz Hanhe, the first director of AIMS, in conversation in the cafeteria

What makes AIMS so compelling, however, is the atmosphere. Fritz Hahne, sitting in an old anorak in the cafeteria, where teachers eat alongside students, described it this way: "This is a different kind of pedagogy, it's not designed to sift and sort people. It is about getting them to grow

and for that you need to get them to learn how to ask interesting, open questions. There is no fixed curriculum. It is not about getting the answers to questions right or wrong. It is about encouraging them to explore and solve problems. So we aim to teach less, but teach better. Interdisciplinary teaching is vital because you want to encourage students to attack problems from different angles." Sessions at AIMS, even those with Nobel prize-winners and international experts, are more like open discussions than lessons. Students learn from one another as well as from their teachers. Eva Lillian contrasted her experience in Rwanda with her time at Muizenberg: "Here you can get really close to teachers, have a conversation with them, about anything." She looks as though she is still getting over the shock.

The examinations too are mainly oral, a process of to and fro, back and forth, testing ideas and asking students to justify their answers. "We don't give them precise marks and grades," explained Barry Green, the director, "because we don't want them to chase grades. It's not about testing knowledge but developing people who are mathematicians and scientists."

The atmosphere at AIMS is like the spirit of a small rural primary school following the Escuela Nueva model and reflects the kind of teaching that is being encouraged by TESSA. Though very different, these three schemes share some core ideas about what makes learning happen. Our innovators are pragmatists: they are driven by what works for their pupils. Yet these pragmatists have shared principles. They want no part in the ideological and theoretical disputes between behaviourists and constructivists, traditionalists and radicals. They want approaches that work and especially for students who are most likely to be turned off by more traditional forms of instruction.

Our innovators share these underlying principles about how effective learning happens:

■ Learning in traditional schools is symbolised by children seated in rows, looking to the teacher at the front of the class, at a blackboard. It is linear, vertical and hierarchical. Most of our innovators gather students in circles, to learn together, from one another as well as a teacher who is a facilitator. Their models are circular, flat and horizontal.

■ Learning is an active process in which people interpret knowledge and adapt it to new contexts and uses. Mastering a subject or a skill is not simply a matter of memorising content nor even of embedding routines (though both play an important part in learning, from multiplication tables and languages to music and sport). Learning comes from acquiring knowledge and being able to apply it in different settings. Learning should be a generative process in which knowledge and understanding grow and adapt, both integrating older knowledge and casting it aside.

■ Engaged learning is impossible unless the learner feels motivated. Learning is often a matter of developing formal, analytical and cognitive skills. But that is impossible without the right kind of motivation which, in turn, raises the emotional dimensions of learning.

■ To be motivating, learning has to feel personally significant. Even if much of the content has elements of standardisation, the experience of learning needs to be per-

LEFT: Professor Barry Green, the current director of AIMS, outside the centre; **BELOW:** One of the centre's staff outside the adjacent research centre, built in refurbished seaside villas

sonalised to make people feel engaged. That implies that provision needs to be flexible enough to meet different needs in different ways. Children should be encouraged to become protagonists in their own learning and given a voice in the process. As people learn more they should be increasingly capable of self-regulating their learning rather than relying on the teacher to regulate the pace and goals of that learning.

■ Personalised learning does not mean solo learning. Learning is an interactive process of dialogue, as much with peers as with teachers. Collaboration has cognitive benefits:

children learn to acknowledge the viewpoints and insights of others; to combine their ideas with others. Learning with other people in the right way can prove hugely motivating.

■ When people face complex tasks it is important they understand underlying principles and how they should be applied in novel contexts. Rather than reaching for the "right" answer they need to adopt the right approach. The more that learning focuses on how to solve complex questions, rather than delivering the right answer to a simple question, the less that teaching can be about the delivery of knowledge.

■ Learning thrives on feedback and not just at the end of the course to test what has been learned. Formative assessment provides more constant feedback, guiding people as they learn. Assessment should be more like creative dialogue than a mark out of ten. Measurable, explicit targets, tests and exams are not so good at capturing tacit, less observable aspects of learning that are social and emotional.

■ Learning needs to be stretching and challenging. Finding the right way to stimulate young people to take on unfamiliar and possibly daunting challenges is one of the keys to good teaching. Setting and meeting low aspirations is an easy way out. The excitement and thrill people feel when they achieve a task they initially thought was beyond them is vital to feed the appetite for learning.

■ Learning should be hard work but rewarding and fun.

RIGHT: Students in a lesson at the Cristo Rey school in Boston, one of 24 in the US network started by Jesuit priests; **TOP:** Emily Smalley, coordinator of the Cristo Rey school, Boston, surrounded by students; **ABOVE:** A Cristo Rey student relaxes during break

It should encourage exploration and discovery but not without a map to help people orient themselves and to find out where they have got to. Even exploratory learning needs a degree of structure.

■ Learning can take place in a wide variety of settings, not just in a school classroom. A range of settings – in the community, in cultural institutions, at work – needs to be utilised.

■ Designing the conditions for this kind of active, engaged, self-reflective learning is a demanding and sophisticated task, much more so than delivering traditional lessons from a blackboard at the front of the class. It takes highly skilled, creative teachers to lead this kind of learning.

These principles are at work in Aprendiz's extension of learning from school into the community; in the collaborative learning amongst mothers encouraged by MOCEP; the computer games provided by Hole in the Wall to make learning fun; the intense, high-level discussions at AIMS; and the collaborative, self-organised learning promoted by Escuela Nueva. At Cristo Rey the classroom teaching might be traditional but much of what children learn comes from their experience at work, where they have to be fleet of foot and work in teams. In Pakistan, The Citizens Foundation is exploring how to integrate critical thinking and creativity into its curriculum. Save the Children endorsed similar principles in their report on the Rewrite the Future campaign: "In countries affected by conflict, a broader set of learning outcomes is arguably particularly important, including critical thinking, practical skills, emotional and social development and attitudes and values that reflect human rights." Among the ingredients of a high quality education, Save the Children lists an education that is relevant to the context children live in; participatory, involving children and their families in learning and the organisation of school; flexible enough to meet changing needs and conditions.

The trouble is that even when children make it to school, learning of this kind is rarely available to them. Professor John Hattie's analysis of more than 800 large-scale studies of learning found that the most effective approach is to engage the learner as a participant: "It is what teachers get the students to do in the class that emerged as the strongest component of the accomplished teachers' repertoire, rather than what the teacher, specifically, does. Students must be actively involved in their learning with a focus on multiple paths to problem-solving." Teachers are successful, Hattie concluded, when they can get their pupils to see the common principles underlying

separate pieces of knowledge and then reconstruct what they know in response to different challenges. What matters is what the students are encouraged to do with the knowledge they have gained rather than what the teacher presents to them. Passive learners may tend to prefer teachers who are highly organised, with clear objectives and highly structured lessons. More active learners prefer enthusiastic, adaptive teachers, prepared to try out different approaches and encourage high levels of interaction in class. "The aim of schooling," Hattie says "should be to maximise the number of active learners, but this requires teachers who can see learning through the eyes of their students and thence know how to engage them in learning that leads to these attributes."

Linda Darling-Hammond, Professor of Education at Stanford University, reaches much the same conclusion, surveying the stubborn inequalities that blight the education of so many African-Americans. Equalising access to educational opportunity means creating more opportunities for meaningful learning, she says. Children are split early into different tracks and streams, she argues, with those labelled difficult or slow deposited in far less challenging lessons. Far less is expected and demanded of them; fewer resources and less time are devoted to them. Not surprisingly they produce exactly what is expected of them: poorer results.

"Education can no longer be productively focused primarily on the transmission of pieces of information that, once memorised, comprise a stable storehouse of knowledge," Darling-Hammond argues. "Instead, schools must teach disciplinary knowledge in ways that focus on central concepts and help students learn how to think critically and learn for themselves, so that they can use knowledge in new situations and manage the demands of changing information, technologies, jobs and social conditions."

The transmission-oriented curriculum was designed to be delivered in large, impersonal, factory-model schools that passed students from one teacher to the next, from year to year, subject to subject, in 50-minute blocks. "Challenging curricula are rationed to a very small proportion of students... Indeed, access to a high-quality curriculum – that is, a combination of ambitious, well-sequenced goals for learning enacted through intellectually challenging assignments, strong instruction and supportive materials – is relatively rare in the United States."

That is the next challenge innovators need to tackle: not who learns and how, but what they learn.

Pictures of Mustafa Kemal
Ataturk are commonplace
in Turkish schools, reflecting
the association between
education and national
development

WHAT: KNOWLEDGE AND CAPABILITIES

Preparing food for the
livestock at the San Francisco
farm school run by Fundación
Paraguaya in Cerrito,
near Asuncion, Paraguay

CLOCKWISE FROM TOP: Martin Burt talking to three pupils returning to school for lunch after a morning learning in the San Francisco farm; a boy leaves the livestock pens to visit the market garden; **LEFT:** One of the few signs that the farm school's founders were Franciscan monks

The relief of an Indian elephant built into a wall is the only clue there is to the eccentric origins of the San Francisco Agriculture School in Cerrito, an hour's drive west from Asunción, Paraguay's capital. The San Francisco Agriculture School was started by Franciscan monks fleeing persecution in India in the 1950s, before being taken over by the De La Salle Brothers in the 1970s. By the turn of the century it was on its last legs as a result of falling numbers and unreliable government funding. In desperation the brothers turned to Martin Burt, the former mayor of Asunción and founder of Fundación Paraguaya, the first microcredit fund in Latin America.

Burt had a track record in risk-taking. He once faced down tanks sent by the federal government by organising his council rubbish trucks to block the capital's main roads. He was also committed to finding solutions to poverty that were built on self-reliance: Fundación Paraguaya has lent more than $97.5m to more than 47,000 microenterprises. The fund's success meant Burt had a surplus to invest when the De La Salle Brothers asked him whether he would take over their beautiful but ailing school, its amber buildings nestling in woods in the *chacos*, the vast agricultural scrubland that stretches all the way into Brazil. Burt saw an opportunity to pursue his mission – to find ways for people to work their way out of poverty – in a different way, through education.

Paraguay's education system is on a par with much of Latin America. There is near universal access to primary education but only 64% of pupils complete the course. In rural areas the number is much lower. Only 60% of children go on to secondary school and among children from the poorest fifth of families the dropout rate is closer to 66%. If you are the child of illiterate, poor parents in a rural village in Paraguay your chances of getting a decent education up to the age of 18 are remote. Martin Burt wanted to change all that.

There is nothing new in the idea of a residential farm school where children learn animal husbandry and crop fertilisation alongside maths and history. What Burt brought was a recipe that had never been tried before: a farm school that could pay for itself by the children selling the produce they grew. To make that possible, what they learned and how they learned had to change.

Educating a student at the school costs about $2,000 a year. To earn the money to pay for the teachers, the students spend one week working – on the organic farm that forms part of the school, or in the school's hotel and restaurant – and then the following week in class. Children cheerfully wander about splattered in mud wearing rubber boots and filthy clothes. They go to school 280 days a year, rather than the 180 in a regular state school. Everyone gets up at 5.45am to clean the school from top to bottom before having breakfast. Then 75 children head off for lessons and the other 75 go to work in the farm. All the students, Burt explains, come from families that scratch out a meagre living on the harsh soil of the chacos, often using techniques that have changed little in 50 years.

Burt reflected, standing next to some cows being milked: "Breaking out of the gravitational pull of poverty is incredibly hard. The problem with farm schools and indeed missionary schools was that they were designed to keep people poor. The most important lesson children learn when they come here is that change is possible. If you graduate from here you aren't poor in skills, confidence and attitude. The poor have tremendous inner resources and capabilities; it's a question of bringing that out of them."

Children do not just emerge from San Francisco with a standard high school diploma. They also get a diploma in a vocational skill and they learn, on the job, how to run a successful business. They do not just earn to learn, they learn while they are earning.

Nilson Acquino, 18, is a prime example. Working with two young boys, Edgar 16 and Pedro 14, he explains patiently how to double dig a vegetable bed so that it can be planted more closely and productively. First he digs out 30cm of topsoil and heaps it on top of the bed. Then he drives his fork into the soil beneath, breaking it up, to make it easier for the roots to penetrate to the moist soil and reach the microbes below. "Farmers need to know how to grow food more efficiently and to charge higher prices," his teacher, Jorge Malineres, himself a graduate of the school explains. In a few months Nilson will follow in his teacher's footsteps to EARTH University in Costa Rica.

All over the school children are collecting eggs and milking cows, slaughtering and plucking chickens, fermenting yoghurt and making cheese. "There is nothing here that is not for real," Burt says. "This is not a project they do on the side, it is not a simulation of a business. It is a business. Every cent counts." In the first year under Burt's leadership San Francisco made just $42,000. Now it makes in excess of $350,000, enough to cover its costs and leave a small surplus.

In the first year under Burt's leadership San Francisco made just $42,000. Now it makes in excess of

$350,000

The school can only promote this kind of active, entrepreneurial learning with a different kind of teaching. When Burt took over, many of the original staff left. He recruited the school's new senior leadership from the microcredit movement because they knew how to run a business on a tight budget. The school's director is responsible for the academic results and the business of balancing its books. The hospitality teacher, Martina Caballero, teaches her subject by running a profitable hotel. San Francisco is an immersive, productive community of learning, in which teachers and pupils work alongside one another, the older children often learning how to run a business by teaching their younger charges.

Burt has set up two more schools in Paraguay, including one deep in the forest which is just for girls. This tiny experiment in an obscure corner of Latin America has excited interest from across the world. The day we visited, the school gathered to say farewell to its director Hugo Florentine, who was moving to Tanzania to set up a network of self-sufficient farm schools. At lunch were a group from Mexico who were planning to emulate the model. What has drawn them to Cerrito is an approach to education which changes the lives of its students. Burt judges his success on the outcomes it makes possible. Within four months of leaving, every graduate will have a job or be in further study.

What children at San Francisco are learning is a set of skills they will need to run their own successful business, to claw their way out of poverty. That content is not set by a national curriculum but by creative responses their teachers have devised to help them meet the challenges they will face as adults, in real life. They will leave with diplomas but really what they are learning is how to escape poverty under their own steam.

"This is not a project they do on the side, it is not a simulation of a business. It is a business. Every cent counts."

Children at the San Francisco school collect eggs and pluck chickens to provide food for the school and to sell in order to pay for their education

CLOCKWISE FROM ABOVE: Two boys take a break from work to drink a cup of *mate*, traditional Paraguayan tea; the farm uses oxen because most of the farms that pupils will work on do not have tractors; the market garden, where most of the school's food is grown; Nilson Acquino tending some young plants; boys resting from milking; Nilson Acquino surveys his plot; girls work alonsgide boys at the farm

What knowledge and skills do children need to be equipped for the twenty-first century? There is widespread agreement that the "factory-era" school system that developed in the twentieth century is inadequate for the century to come. That kind of schooling teaches children compliance and punctuality; obedience and the ability to follow instructions; how to memorise the right answers and regurgitate them on cue. There is far less agreement about what should take its place.

Critics such as Sir Ken Robinson have built a worldwide reputation by advocating a more personalised approach, with an emphasis on the creativity that standard schools stifle. Robinson's position is echoed by those who take their lead from the demands of employers in the globally-connected, innovation-driven economy, which requires workers who are flexible, adaptable and able to solve problems cooperatively. This is creating what Tony Wagner, Professor of Education at Harvard University, calls the global achievement gap: "The gap between what even our best suburban, urban and rural public schools are teaching and testing, versus what all students will need to succeed as learners, workers and citizens in today's global knowledge economy." Modern education, Wagner argues, should be organised around interesting questions children should explore, rather than the answers they should memorise to get top marks in exams. The whole idea of a curriculum is outdated.

Wagner's analysis is endorsed by many global businesses, especially in the high tech sector, who have promoted the idea of twenty-first century skills: communication, critical thinking, collaboration and creativity. About 70% of US jobs require specialised knowledge and skills, compared with just 5% at the dawn of the twentieth century, when the foundations for mass public education were laid. The modern economy is increasingly unwilling and unable to absorb untrained, manual labour, which the school system produces in large quantities. The new mission of schools should be to prepare children to work in jobs that do not exist, to solve problems that are not yet apparent, using technologies that are still to be invented, according to Linda Darling-Hammond. That means equipping them with the ability to apply and reapply knowledge in inventive ways. In a nutshell: collaborative creativity should be at the heart of modern education rather than the culture of compliance of schools in the industrial era.

Yet this new orthodoxy has run into its own critics, both liberal and conservative. One of the most stringent has been Eric Donald Hirsch, a former Yale professor of literature, who argues that these new skills of communication, cooperation and creativity depend on mastering content, primarily aspects of basic underlying knowledge. It is difficult for children to learn how to interpret history without learning some basic facts, dates and events. Hirsch's position has been tacitly endorsed by governments moving towards more prescriptive, detailed curricula that specify what children should know at each stage of their education. Critics of a more liberal bent object that the focus on skills with an economic pay-off is too instrumental: it sells education short. Martha Nussbaum, the Harvard University ethics professor, argues in *Cultivating Humanity* and *Not for Profit: Why Democracy Needs the Humanities*, that education should be based on classical ideals and a respect for the humanities, especially in a world awash with consumerism, commerce and technology. Meanwhile Howard Gardner, the Harvard educationalist famous for his idea that intelligence comes in multiple forms, argues that education should promote the classical virtues of truth, beauty and goodness.

What do our innovators have to say about this increasingly tangled, fraught debate? What do they think children should learn?

Computers can transform education, but many poorer schools in the developing world lack even electricity and so rely on older tools and methods

Our innovators work in societies at very different levels of economic and democratic development, from blasted inner city neighbourhoods in the developed world, to slums in the developing world, to remote rural villages. What stands out is the sheer diversity of what children need to learn to cope with life where they live. For a girl growing up in a slum in Africa, learning how not to become HIV-positive may be the most important knowledge and skill she can gain. In rural Paraguay, learning how to make the most of your topsoil might be vital. In inner-city Chicago, learning how to resist the temptations of gangs and drugs and stay the course to college might be the crucial skill. Perhaps the biggest danger is that children are forced to follow a curriculum that is too rigid and too distant from their lives. Our innovators are focusing on some common areas where skill and knowledge are combined.

The first big theme is globalisation. There is a growing convergence around common skills needed to access jobs in the global economy: reading, writing and comprehension in a world language, like English or Spanish; basic computer skills; an understanding of maths and science; social skills to get on with other people.

The growing importance of global interconnections raises other issues. One is how people cope with cultural difference and diversity. An example of cross-cultural education is The 99, a comic strip and animated cartoon series created by Dr Naif Mutawa, based on the 99 attributes of Allah, ranging from generosity to learning, and designed to counter extremist versions of Islam around the world. The 99, which is moving onto television and online, is drawn by artists that Dr Mutawa recruited from Marvel and who used to work on Spiderman. In Bosnia, Serbia, and Croatia, history teachers have taken a brave initiative to open a discussion about how their shared history of conflict should be taught. The Connect Programme, Soliya, uses video conferencing technology to connect young people around the world, something the UN University for Peace has been doing for three decades. Another issue is how education helps people to enrich the cultures they come from, to protect them against being flattened by a steamroller of common, global culture of television and music. In the late nineteenth and early twentieth century education systems were tools of national unification, creating common knowledge and culture, projecting national pride and economic prowess. Now education systems need to adapt to a world of continuous and intense global interconnectedness.

The second theme is sustainability. Mass public schooling systems were both a product of industrialisation and a means to drive it. Children leaving school now enter a world facing the threat of growing disruption from possibly extreme climate change. Innovators are responding by devising new ways to integrate sustainability into education, to help students learn how to frame and solve problems of energy, transport and waste in new and more effective ways. That stretches from the Enviro-Protect biodiversity project in Cameroon, to sustainable tourism in Guatemala (Asociación Ak'Tenamit), to the University of Tennessee's Living Light challenge to design a light source which only consumes as much energy as it produces, and the world's first College of Sustainability, at Dalhousie University in Canada, which has created a cross-disciplinary programme drawing together biology, physics, environmental, social and economic sciences.

The third theme is citizenship and self-governance. Our innovators operate in every kind of democracy, from the established to the fragile, from societies that are secular to those where the state promotes religion. Yet across the range, people see education as the route to self-governance and responsible citizenship. Education is both feeding and being fed by this democratic, everyday culture, which changes how people expect to be treated by those in power.

Finally, our innovators are reconnecting learning to work. The connection between earning and learning is central to Martin Burt's burgeoning global network of self-financing farm schools. Many other projects are based on the idea that the ultimate test of someone's education is whether it leads them into productive work. They also fear that schools are in danger of becoming too academic and detached from real life. One of the common remedies is to forge closer links between business and education.

In Turkey, Europe's fastest-growing economy, more than a fifth of young people under the age of 20 are unemployed and yet employers complain that they cannot find the right people to fill their vacancies. In 2006, KOC, one of the oldest and largest companies in Turkey, launched a $20m, seven-year programme, to support 8,000 students at 256 vocational schools for four years. The students have to promise to continue their vocational education and to behave like a potential KOC employee. They get a small scholarship as an incentive, and a mentor from a KOC company to help them prepare for work. Education for Employment runs a similar programme across much of the Arab world supported by leading local and international businesses such as Cisco and Carrefour. The programme's Jordanian affiliate, JCEF, for example, has developed courses in hospitality, retail, information technology and sales, providing young people with a route to learn the skills they need to get their first job and to start a career.

Our innovators do not see much mileage in engaging with polarised academic and political debates about twenty-first century skills. They take a much more pragmatic view on how knowledge and skills, content and capability, develop in tandem. Learning can be structured and sequential and yet also encourage creativity and proceed through interaction. Many of the innovations we have seen have a deliberate structure which sets out what needs to be learned: MOCEP's step-by-step guide for mothers to be educators; TESSA's templated modules for teaching training; Escuela Nueva's learning guides for children. Yet these projects also encourage learning as a highly participative and dynamic activity. The skills of critical thinking and creativity are not new. These skills may now be in more demand than they were. But as with so much innovation it may be a case of combining the old with the new: old-fashioned skills with new technologies; content with capabilities.

Perhaps the biggest danger is that whatever curriculum a system adopts it becomes too detailed and prescriptive. Imagine for a moment sitting down in 1911 to set out the skills children would need in the decades to come. Who then would have been able to predict the rise of the mass automobile, the television, two World Wars and one Cold War, the atomic bomb, communism and fascism, Mao and Pol Pot, computers, the contraceptive pill and Elvis? Claims to be able to predict in detail what children need to learn to prosper in the century to come need to be treated with caution.

The most successful education systems – in Finland and Singapore for example – have curricula that are relatively light on prescription, so students devote more time to deeper learning around a smaller number of topics. Limited core curricula allow teachers more scope to adapt how they teach. As John Hattie concludes in his international survey *Visible Learning*, what a curriculum says is less important than what a teacher can do with it. Part of the problem is that students can easily be confused by material that is too difficult for them but bored by material they already know. How children are taught and what they are taught need to go together. Getting that combination right is the key to the final big issue our innovators address: motivating students to learn.

Cards that help children learn
to read, at NM Joshi Municipal
School in Mumbai, India

CHAPTER 7

WHY: COMPELLING NOT COMPULSORY

Students and parents arrive
for a celebration of success
at the Pathways to Education
project in Regent Park, Toronto

Carolyn Acker was frustrated. She had been working on a community health project in Regent Park, one of the oldest and poorest public housing estates in Canada for five years, and had made barely any impact on the cycles of deprivation and illness that blighted the lives of its residents, mostly recent immigrants. Regent Park was built in 1948 as a model project, with houses around closed courtyards and a series of modern tower blocks: streets in the sky they called them. Originally home to Irish and Italian immigrants, Regent Park then received waves of Tamil, Bengali, Vietnamese and Sudanese. By then it had also become a haven for drug-dealers. In the year 2000 it hit rock bottom: there were nine murders in one small housing project.

That summer persuaded Acker she had to change tack. The place was going down the drain, taking its young people with it. Acker decided the best way to improve the community's health was to get more of its young people into higher education and from there into better jobs. Their incomes would rise and their health would improve. Yet when Acker examined Regent Park's educational performance the picture looked just as bleak. Most of the residents had travelled half-way around the world looking for work and opportunity. The parents were hardworking, determined and enterprising. Yet their children's performance at school was little more than disastrous. At the age of 14 four in ten children from Regent Park were passing their grades in only two subjects, an early warning sign of impending failure. Sure enough, 56% of Regent Park's children dropped out before completing secondary school. Only a fifth went on to post-secondary education. Children who drop out of school are twice as likely to be unemployed as adults.

Acker and her colleague Norman Rowen began talking to parents and children about how to turn the situation around. What they found was that children wanted to go to school. The parents wanted their children to become doctors and nurses. But they all found the secondary education system daunting and confusing. Many of the parents could not speak English and had not completed secondary schooling in the country they came from. Many were in dead-end, low-paid jobs which meant they had to work all hours to make ends meet. They had little time to help their children study. Getting to secondary school meant travelling by bus, which was beyond the means of many of the poorest families. Going to college was beyond their wildest dreams. At school the children found it all too easy to play up to the stereotypes many of their teachers seemed to have of them, condemning them to a damning cycle of low aspirations, expectations and outcomes. When Rowen went to one school to talk to the teachers about how to do better by the difficult kids from Regent Park, the vice principal replied: "These kids? Why bother?"

LEFT: Carolyn Acker with a former student of Pathways to Education, who is now studying for a master's degree; **BELOW:** Pathways to Education co-founder, Norman Rowen

Rowen talked to more than 200 young people and their parents, building up a detailed picture of the many obstacles that blocked their path to college. She also talked to a small number of young people who had escaped from Regent Park to get to college. Each of them said their success was due to having a powerful and committed mentor – a teacher, sports coach, priest – who stood by them.

From these disparate ingredients Acker and Rowen designed a simple yet comprehensive programme for all young people from Regent Park at secondary school. The programme, which became Pathways to Education, is based on a deal. This is how it works.

Once a child enrols on the programme they get a free bus pass to travel to and from school. Each year that the child is on the programme $1,000 is deposited in an account towards the costs of university tuition. To claim those benefits the child has to attend school at least 85% of the time and they have to get the credits they need to move to the next stage of education. Pathways gives children intensive support to make sure they make it. Children have to attend homework sessions that are run four evenings a week in a local community centre staffed by volunteers. A couple of times a month they go to see volunteer mentors in the community – doctors, lawyers, teachers – who will link them to opportunities to work. Crucially each is allocated a support worker, to act as their mentor and to liaise with parents and school. The support worker is like a personal trainer, but for schoolwork: motivating, supporting, setting higher targets, building strengths in areas of weakness.

Acker explained: "The support worker is vital. They are not teachers, nor are they social workers. They come from around here. They provide tough love. We want to build up a sense of discipline in these kids, an internal guidance system so they do not give in to the immediate urge but invest in the longer term."

Pathways got going in 2001, the year after the Regent Park murders, with the help of funding from some far-sighted foundations. The impact was almost immediate. About 95% of eligible children enrolled in the programme. Only 11% of Regent Park children now do not make their grades at 14. The dropout rate has fallen from 56% to 15%. A study by Boston Consulting Group suggests a dollar invested in Pathways yields a 24-fold return across a lifetime, in terms of higher incomes, taxes and lower public spending. Eight out of ten children who complete the Pathways programme go onto further education, most of them to university.

Kalvin Chan is a classic example. Kalvin's parents did not complete secondary school but that was in Shanghai. When they arrived in Canada, speaking barely any English, Kalvin's father worked in a car assembly factory and his mother in textiles. Kalvin arrived in Regent Park just as it turned sour. His parents, he says, were very good at hiding how poor the family was. Kalvin enrolled in Pathways in eighth grade but to begin with, the programme made little impression on him. He was barely scraping through. The turning point came when he told his teacher that he wanted to go to college to study to become a paramedic. She smiled condescendingly and advised him to lower his sights to manual jobs he would be able to get with his mediocre grades. When Kalvin

relayed that conversation to his Pathways support worker he was told he could get the grades he needed, and he could even do an internship at a local hospital, but he had to get his act together. And that is exactly what Kalvin did. He started putting some effort into school, attending the homework classes and taking note of what his peers were doing. Kalvin did make it to college and he now works, as a paramedic, at the hospital where his support worker organised his first internship.

The success of the Regent Park programme attracted further foundation funding and eventually a government investment of $5m a year for four years to take the programme all over Canada. By 2011 Pathways was serving 3,380 students in 11 communities. By 2016 it aims to be serving close to 10,000 students in twenty projects. David Hughes, the chief executive of the Pathways Foundation, established to oversee the foundation's scaling efforts, estimates there are 75,000 students in Canada, mainly from ethnic minority backgrounds, who could benefit from the programme.

Pathways does not change what children learn at school, nor how they are taught. It does not involve any radical departures in pedagogy. What Acker and Rowen have created is a motivation machine to keep students wanting to learn even when the going gets tough. That motivation is partly extrinsic and immediate: the offer of a free bus pass which they can use to get around town and not just to go to school. The incentives are also deferred, teaching them to wait for a pay-off: the fund that is waiting for them when they start college. But just as important are the social spurs they get, from peers, support workers and mentors, and the kick they get from doing well at school.

> Only 11% of Regent Park children now do not make their grades at 14. The drop out rate has fallen from 56% to 15%

Children play in the church parking lot in Regent Park, Toronto. In the background new apartments are the first signs of the physical regeneration of the estate

If children go through a full course of primary and secondary education they should spend six hours a day, 220 days a year, for 15 years in school. But if too many of those hours are passed in draining boredom, their curiosity left dormant and their imaginations unengaged, with no clear idea of where their teacher is leading them and why, then it should be little wonder that children switch off, look out of the window, grow distracted and disenchanted.

There is a widespread assumption that the biggest challenges are on the supply-side of education: if we can just get more children into school for longer then everything should sort itself out. We assume that most parents want their children to be at school and that most children want to go. Yet many of the most significant challenges we face may be on the demand side: parents and children do not invest in education because they see little point in doing so. It could be that it's their low aspirations that lead to low attendance and poor outcomes.

One version of this view, advocated by economists, is that people see education as an investment. People will send their children to school, so the story goes, only if they can see a clear return. They are prepared to put in time and effort, and forgo the wages they might earn, in exchange for higher earnings later in life once they have left school. People might rationally calculate that it does not make sense to invest in education because they can only see low returns, because there are not enough jobs that pay higher sums for those with an education. The rewards are too distant and uncertain to make the investment worth it.

These calculations are a crucial factor for parents in parts of India. Abhijit Banerjee and Esther Duflo describe in *Poor Economics* a study that shows that when firms running international call centres started recruiting in remote villages, parents started sending their daughters to school in higher numbers. Several of our innovators have designed programmes with this investment model in mind. Cristo Rey schools, for example, are based on a clear pitch that they aim to get children into good paying jobs while they are at school and into colleges that will give them successful careers. The San Francisco Agriculture School motivates children to learn because it offers them a route out of poverty.

Economic incentives, however, are only one part of the complicated story of what motivates – and demotivates – students.

Even if children are looking for a clear pay-off from school, they may not be thinking in terms of their future employment prospects. As Clayton Christensen and his colleagues argue, understanding student motivation means stepping into their shoes: "They want to feel successful and make progress and they want to have fun with friends." If doing well at school helps young people achieve these two basic goals in life – doing well and being popular – then they will go to school. If going to school spells, boredom, failure, anxiety, bullying and potential humiliation, then it should be no surprise that young people turn to other activities that offer them a better chance of feeling successful and popular: music, sport, gangs, work. Or alternatively they might simply choose to hide themselves, tucked into a corner at the back of the class, hoping not to be spotted.

Schools are competing in the "attention" economy. State mandated education systems face direct competition from private schools, but their real competition is for the attention of their students, who have a growing range of other distracting possibilities in their lives. Social media, video games, software that allows them to create music and animation, all feed children's sense that they can enjoy, share, talk and do, all at the same time, often connected to friends. Schools rarely create that rich mix of experiences for children. That is why schools find it hard to hold their attention.

Moreover, the decisions that people make about learning are rarely based on rational calculations, as economists imagine. Learning is often a highly-charged activity: it involves challenges and failures, setbacks and triumphs, as children overcome obstacles and solve problems. Those challenges excite emotions ranging from elation to humiliation and depression. When children feel negative emotions they are more likely to disinvest from learning. Monique Boekaerts from Leiden University in the Netherlands, an expert in the emotional aspects of learning, argues children feel positive emotions when they feel competent and in control, are self-regulating and yet also working well with their peers. Children are more likely to feel positive about a challenge if they feel they have the resources to complete it successfully. That makes them open to new ideas and feedback; they become more playful and energised. If students fear they will lose face and be shown up by their lack of knowledge they become more closed and defensive, unwilling to accept feedback and averse to taking risks.

Large, anonymous, impersonal, system-driven secondary schools which pass children in batches along an educational conveyor belt seem designed to deny children the personal

An empty secondary school
in Sao Paulo waits for summer
to end and students to return

"[...] then it should be little wonder that children switch off, look out of the window, grow distracted and disenchanted."

support and encouragement they need to feel good about learning. That is why Pathways to Education provides pupils with a support worker to act as a surrogate parent, coach and mentor. Yet relationships with adults are probably less important than the peer influences children come under: what their friends are doing and whether learning is regarded as cool. That is why good schools are often like communities in which students encourage and support one another.

Perhaps the most important factor that draws people back to learning is that it can be a rewarding and enjoyable experience: it is intrinsically rather than socially or economically rewarding. As cognitive scientist Daniel Willingham argues in *Why Don't Students Like School?* efforts to make lessons seem relevant and feel contemporary will not work for long. Students will see through such superficial devices. Relevant content is far less important, Willingham shows, than how pupils are invited to engage with it, what they can make of it. The most rewarding and exciting learning often involves subjects that go well beyond a pupil's everyday experiences and which stretch their imaginations. It does not have to be relevant to their everyday life. To be motivating, learning has to be meaningful for students. They have to see where what they have learned fits into what they already know and what the point might be. Learning has to excite people's curiosity but then help them safely navigate their way across the unfamiliar terrain. Nor does it count for much, Willingham says, if a teacher is nice, personable and tells good jokes only for their lessons to be poorly-organised, badly-planned and without a clear purpose: "The brilliantly well-organised teacher whom fourth graders see as mean will not be very effective. But the funny teacher, or the gentle storytelling teacher, whose lessons are poorly organised won't be much good either. Effective teachers have both qualities. They are able to connect personally with students, and they organise the material in a way that makes it interesting and easy to understand." That philosophy is at the heart of one of our other innovators, the IMC Weekend School in the Netherlands, created by Heleen Terwijn.

> Effective teachers have both qualities. They are able to connect personally with students, and they organize the material in a way that makes it interesting and easy to understand.

Terwijn, a psychologist at the University of Amsterdam, was researching the high rates of unemployment and crime amongst the Surinamese community in the south of the city, when she came across a puzzle. The teenagers she met were downbeat, demoralised, demotivated and about a quarter of them were depressed. They seemed to have no faith in their ability to shape their future and could see little point in going to schools that seemed designed to channel them into a dead end. Yet the same children at the age of 10 were engaged, excited, hopeful: they believed anything was possible. What was it, Terwijn wondered, that changed, usually between the age of 10 and 13, to so demoralise these children?

The heart of the problem is that, at the age of 12, children in the Netherlands sit an exam which determines which of five kinds of secondary school they will enter. In general only students from the top two academic streams make it into higher education. Extreme motivation is required for a student to work their way out of one stream and into another. Once these bright, open and energetic children find themselves confined to one of the lower academic streams the world closes in on them. They see little point in learning and they are given precious little encouragement to do so.

Terwijn hit upon a solution which involved reinventing an old idea: the Sunday school. Modern mass education systems in Europe can trace their roots to Sunday schools set up by churches in the eighteenth and nineteenth century. Terwijn decided she would set up a Sunday school with a twist: a place where children from the poorest backgrounds could meet and be taught on short courses run by professionals passionate about their field – doctors, vets, lawyers, advertising executives, designers. If the students could feel the passion of these professionals, have their horizons opened up and see how learning connects to the real world, that might motivate them to learn, Terwijn figured.

Terwijn completed her university research in December 1997 and devised the plan for the first Weekend School on the back of an envelope. She was lucky enough, through a friend, to meet Rob Defares, the managing director of a trading company IMC, who stumped up the money for the first school, which Terwijn opened with 30 students in January 1998. After a lengthy period of trial and error, Terwijn honed her model. This is how it works.

Each Weekend School is open every Sunday during the school term for about 100 children from three school years, from schools in the lowest tier of the secondary education system. The Weekend Schools take place in borrowed offices and buildings, some loaned by universities, others by companies. Each school has three staff to plan the programme and look after each year group. Those staff organize a roster of guest and volunteer

Heleen Terwijn (**TOP LEFT**), founder of the IMC Weekend School network in the Netherlands, and young people who come to the Weekend School to take part in collaborative and creative projects that introduce them to new disciplines and increase their motivation for learning, led by tutors who are usually professionals in fields such as advertising, the law and medicine

teachers who run classes and help students with their school work. The point, Terwijn says, is for children to be able to navigate their own paths in life. But that is easier said than done: "I loathe projects that think if they take kids to the concert hall they will say 'Oh! I will go forever because I suddenly fell in love with classical music!' I mean, come on, that's not how it works. We are talking about the way that kids give form and shape to their lives and how we can help sustain that."

The Weekend School aims to add motivational spice to the dull educational diet these children endure. Weekend School is designed to be fun. It involves practical work and often a visit to someone's workplace: the zoo to see a zookeeper at work; a court to see a judge. By introducing them to aspirational role models, the School helps to broaden their horizons, as Melle Dotinga, an advertising executive and one of the guest teachers explained: "If you live in an area like these children live in, you don't meet people in professions. Your view on your possibilities in the world is very limited. What Weekend School does is help children discover that there are so many more possibilities." Weekend School students, the evaluations show, have more sense of agency and control over their lives than their peers, and so, Terwijn maintains, they are more likely to want to carry on learning.

Others agree. Terwijn took her time to iron out all the kinks in her model. When she was ready to expand it took almost two years to find her second sponsor, IBM. That gave her the credibility to approach other corporate sponsors. There are nine Weekend Schools in cities across the Netherlands and about 30 schools that emulate the model. The Weekend School, like Pathways to Education, does not change what is taught at school, nor how it is done: what the two programmes add is the catalyst of motivation. They are like outboard motors, added onto the system to propel it forward.

The great strength of state education systems is that they can mandate that children should go to school. As a result they do not have to worry about marketing, advertising or sales. Schools open their doors and children have to come. The weakness of state education is the flip side of this: as a result these systems pay too little attention to what motivates children to learn. Too many children can be physically present but psychologically absent. Innovations to motivate children to learn are as important as hot chilli is to a spicy curry. Take it away and you're left with something very bland.

Young boys relax at the end of a session at the Weekend School, which aims to motivate children to continue learning even when they have been deposited in lower grades at school

"We are talking about the way that kids give form and shape to their lives [...]"

Weekend School, Amsterdam

CHAPTER 8

THE COMBINATION: MORE, BETTER AND DIFFERENT

Crows fly from the field
at the San Francisco farm
school in Cerrito, Paraguay

It is a great achievement that so many more children have been enrolled in school in the last decade: girls as well as boys; the very poor as well as the middle class; those living in distant rural villages as well as city kids; speakers of local and indigenous languages as well as those who speak English and Spanish; the offspring of recent migrants as well as longstanding residents; children brought up in zones of conflict as well as those living in relative peace. As we have seen, even creating equality of access to education requires innovation because children have so many different obstacles to overcome.

But getting children into school is just the first step. Going to school will not make much difference to their lives if they emerge having learned very little. Worse, the experience may have turned them off learning altogether. Too many children are in that position. That is especially likely if they are sat in rows in relatively poor schools, with poorly-trained, paid, managed and motivated teachers, drilling them in an academic curriculum the children barely grasp. In those circumstances, it should be little surprise that as enrolment rates go up so do the dropout and failure rates, as children become bored and demoralized. The prospect of going to school excites hope; the experience all too often delivers disappointment.

That is why so many of our pioneers are devising more engaging, collaborative and participatory approaches to learning. The key is "combinatory innovation" that expands access to education while simultaneously improving its quality and motivating children to learn. More education of the standard kind is not the solution; more needs to be combined with better and different.

Pathways to Education gets the poorest inner-city children in Canada into college by giving them a bundle of incentives to do better. A different approach to motivating students delivers better results and gets more children through the system. Nanhi Kali does much the same with girls in India by providing them with support to maintain their sense of confidence. TESSA is training teachers so more children in Africa can go to school. But it is also encouraging more interactive forms of teaching that engage children as participants. TESSA offers more and better education because it is creating a different approach. Escuela Nueva is doing the same thing: allowing more children to attend better rural schools by employing a different pedagogy, based on a collaborative and self-paced approach. Fundación Paraguaya's San Francisco farm has crea-

ted a way to get better education to more poor children in rural areas by adopting a radically different model: a financially self-sufficient one. Cristo Rey has adopted a similar approach in the United States. The Shafallah Center in Doha has shown that it is possible to deliver equality of access to education for disabled children, but only if schools create highly personalized programmes. The Hole in the Wall in India gives children access to education through computer-based games, which also make for a more playful experience.

The message from these programmes is that to get more children learning in ways that are better for them, education has to be different. Wider access to education needs to be combined with innovations that change how children learn, what they learn and why. Our pioneers achieve their high impact because they create ways to deliver more, better and different kinds of education all at the same time. It's time to look a little more closely at where these innovations come from, how they develop and grow to scale.

Equalising access to schooling only meets the challenge when it also gives children access to exciting, challenging and engaging opportunities to learn

"The prospect of going to school excites hope; the experience all too often delivers disappointment."

CHAPTER 9

INSPIRATION IN THE MARGINS

Most radical innovation starts in the margins. Aprendiz's programme to promote community-based learning started with a public art project to transform this square and alleyway, which was once frequented by drug-dealers

The alley where Aprendiz
started its work covers
the course of a stream.
The murals have been
repainted several times
but never vandalised

An alley mainly frequented by drug dealers, in an area close to the heart of one of the most violent cities in the world, is an unlikely place to start an educational innovation that is driving change in one of the world's largest, fastest-growing economies. Yet that is precisely where Aprendiz started life: in Vila Madalena, a downtown area of São Paulo, Brazil.

In the 1990s São Paulo had an unparalleled reputation for drugs, kidnapping and assassination. So much so that by the end of the decade many residents were afraid to go out, to talk in the street, to sit in parks or visit the cinema. Instead people were busy building high walls around their homes, installing security gates and mentally, if not quite physically, barricading themselves in.

In 1997, in Vila Madelena, an area wedged between São Paulo's trendy downtown and a large favela, a group of journalists and architects decided they had had enough. They wanted to reclaim public spaces for everyday life. One of the first places in which they took a stand was a small alley and adjoining square used only by drug-dealers and their clients. The tools the group used were children and murals. Over several days renowned São Paulo street artists worked with children, from both the favela and nearby middle-class areas, to transform the alley into an outdoor gallery. Since then, the alley has been repainted several times but it has never been vandalised. During the day it is quiet, almost like the nave of a church. For Aprendiz it has a special significance.

The murals in the alley helped to kick off a sustained and daring effort to show that communities can become as important as schools, as places where children learn. At the end of the murals project the team realised the children did not want to leave; they wanted more. Unwittingly they had hit upon the idea that activities out of school, in the community, could help children learn. Aprendiz's goal is neither to paint walls, nor just to transform public spaces. Its aim is to mobilise communities to help children learn. As the founder Gilberto Dimenstein puts it: "The art of educating is too complex and too great to relegate its activities to the boundaries of school."

Aprendiz got started when Dimenstein, a well-known journalist with the São Paulo newspaper *Folha de São Paulo*, returned from a trip to the United States excited by the way the internet was changing how people communicate. He initiated a project to link the elite Bandeirantes school to three nearby public schools, using the web to bring children together when their parents would not let them meet face to face. Out of this initiative came the idea that by learning how to create websites the children could also help Brazil's fledgling non-profits. Bringing children together online provided the spark for a project to bring them together in real life. Sponsored by the mayor of São Paulo the 100 Walls programme put children together with artists to create murals on public walls throughout the city. After that they turned to São Paulo's street artists and that led to the street art project in the alley. It was then that the team realised their main goal was to make the community a locus for learning.

To cut a long story short the experiment in the alley spawned one of the most influential and innovative NGOs in Brazil. The websites have morphed into Aprendiz's own site, dedicated to news and information about education, which employs seven journalists and gets more than 10,000 hits a day. Aprendiz has turned its community arts projects into a "social technology", a systematic way for communities to create learning neighbourhoods. Aprendiz, which is funded by donations that Brazilian companies can offset against tax, works with communities to bring them together to analyse and understand their needs and their capabilities, their weaknesses and their assets. The aim is to show how squares, alleys, shops, companies, cinemas, theatres, dance studios, parks and sports centres can be used for learning. Helena Singer, who leads Aprendiz's education programmes, explained: "This is education as a process of community self-development and control. If we just talked to people about school and education not many would get involved because they see that as the job of teachers. But if we talk, and listen to them, about what they want for their community and their children, then many more will come to talk."

By packaging its social technology in ways that others can use, Aprendiz's influence has spread. Mayors in 30 Brazilian cities, including Rio de Janeiro, have created Learning Neighbourhoods and Community Pedagogues, who are employed by schools, parent-teacher associations or even companies to promote learning in communities. The Federal Government created a More Education programme to spread the Learning Neighbourhoods through community programmes in more than 10,000 schools. Aprendiz has trained 10,700 educators in its methods. Aprendiz, which has more than 100 staff and is currently running more than 40 projects, has become a persistent source of new ideas and innovation, on the edge of the formal school system. This all started in a scruffy alley.

"The art of educating is too complex and too great to relegate its activities to the boundaries of school."

Aprendiz is not alone in its unlikely beginnings. Escuela Nueva started in the poorest rural schools in Colombia, which was then riven by drugs wars. The Citizens Foundation's first school was in Karachi's poorest slum. Martin Burt's movement of self-financing farm schools started in a near bankrupt school in the middle of tiny, land-locked Paraguay, one of the most isolated countries in the world. Turkey's Mother Child Education Program (MOCEP) started life in a pre-school run by a Turkish textile company that was on the verge of going bust. Neil Turok and Fritz Hahne started the African Institute of Mathematics in a run-down 1930s hotel in a surfing resort outside Cape Town, miles from the nearest university.

Harsh conditions often breed radical innovation because innovators starved of resources have no option but to discard traditional, relatively high-cost models. The world-famous child-centred early years programme created in the Italian city of Reggio Emilia, which has inspired a worldwide movement of emulators, started in the chaotic aftermath of World War Two when the Italian education system was barely functioning. Similar conditions led to the creation of one of the most remarkable educational organisations in the Arab world, the Tamer Institute, which started in 1989 during the first Palestinian intifada when widespread school and university closures pushed the community to find ways to compensate for the loss of formal education. Renad Qubbaj, the current director, recalled: "We would find many people would volunteer to open their houses to educate children, or a teacher would meet his students at a mosque or at a church to continue the education process that he or she had started with their students." Out of that grassroots response arose the idea of an organisation that, according to Qubbaj, would empower people with the skills and knowledge to respond to what was happening around them. The Institute takes its name from the *tamer*, the vessel that is used to take seeds from one date tree to another to fertilize them. The Tamer Institute aims to fertilise young people by taking knowledge from place to place. The date is considered a fruit that is both spiritual and something even the poorest can afford: that is what Tamer has tried to replicate with education. Tamer's approach was disarmingly simple: to create community libraries where children aged 6–12 could gather twice a week, to read and listen to stories. The organisation's main tool, Qubbaj says, is the story. Tamer employs about 40 people to run 120 community and school libraries with scores of partners across the West Bank and Gaza. Tamer's flagship programme is the National Reading Campaign and the reading passport, which involved 100,000 children in 2010/2011.

Each of our high impact innovators got started in a particular place, and by and large, those places were at the margins, in difficult, poor and under-resourced areas where innovation and improvisation was the only way to survive. It's with good reason that radical innovation starts in these sorts of places.

Incumbent, mainstream organisations have a strong tendency to reinvest in the assets and infrastructure they have built up, to protect their position. Established and successful organisations have routines that are difficult to budge, entrenched ways of understanding their customers and their jobs. That is why these often successful organisations tend to reinvest in what made them successful in the first place. The task of challenging deeply embedded conventional wisdom is fraught with risk and potential conflict. It is not for the faint-hearted. It makes sense for people in these organisations to play it safe. Radical innovation that threatens conventional operating models is too risky to contemplate, even if it promises big returns. Those factors often make big organisations risk-averse compared to small start-ups. But the problems are even greater in educational bureaucracies: civil servants do not want to take risks and innovation is rarely the route to promotion; teachers and their unions can often be resistant to change; parents can be understandably cautious about risks being taken with their children's schooling; politicians are wary of losing control. The result is that mainstream education systems tend to be risk-averse and when change comes it tends to arrive through sweeping policy changes driven from the centre.

That is why, as Clayton Christensen found in his study *The Innovator's Dilemma*, radical innovation rarely starts with the industry leaders. Invariably it comes from upstarts and outsiders, often starting in marginal markets, with simple, low-cost products, aimed at attracting fresh customers. These upstarts are initially easy to overlook because they start outside the mainstream in an alley in Vila Madalena, a slum in Karachi, a tiny rural school in Colombia, a computer in a slum in Hyderabad, a near-bankrupt farm school. Innovation may come from the best-resourced, newest schools or even university research departments, but we have found that it often starts in the most unlikely places where resources are scarce and so innovators have to devise new solutions. That is just one reason to rethink how innovation happens.

Conventional accounts of innovation have been heavily influenced by the way science and technology was applied to manufacturing in the twentieth century. The iconic figure in that story is Thomas Edison, the inventor of the light bulb and the record player, who still holds the largest number of US patents given to a single individual. Edison set out to create a factory for innovation, systematising the process of creating technologies and turning them into new products. That inspired the idea, taken up for example in the pharmaceuticals industry, that innovation flows down a pipeline from research at one end to consumers at the other. The pipeline view of innovation is that ideas get created at one end by special people working in special places: the boffins in the lab, the designers in their studio. Those ideas are then embedded in physical products, which are manufactured and distributed to consumers waiting at the other end of the pipeline. In the pipeline model consumers play a very limited role in innovation. The implication of this pipeline view is that innovation is synonymous with research and development and is focused on turning science and technology into tangible products. Innovation is presented as a linear series of events – from invention through to eventual use – in an orderly process that connects inventors to users. The main measures of innovative activity are inputs: the amount spent on R&D and the numbers of scientists employed – and formal outputs: scientific papers and patents.

This pipeline model is not much help, however, in explaining how innovation happens in a people-intensive service industry like education, in which competition is limited and the state plays a large role. Most innovation in education does not involve new technologies so much as social technologies: people working together in new ways. New technologies alone rarely produce innovation. It depends on how they are combined with consumer, business and social innovation. The innovation of mountain biking, for example, involved not just new bikes but accessories, clubs, magazines and also new places to cycle catered for by specialist tour operators. The mountain bike is not just a physical innovation: it has helped to create a lifestyle economy. The idea for the mountain bike did not come from researchers working in labs for bike manufacturers. It came from avid off-road bike riders who were frustrated with the bikes they had and wanted to create new ones. They took matters into their own hands by making their own bikes, known as clunkers, which eventually provided the template for the mountain bike. Some of the most disruptive innovations start with consumers and flow back up the pipeline to producers. Even when a product does emerge from a mixture

of design and research it often only comes to life with the help of consumers. Apple developed its app store for the iPhone only after discontented users started hacking the phone's software to add useful applications. Innovation is highly collaborative and interactive, involving a wide range of players and a great deal of toing and froing, as ideas are tested and iterated, not least by consumers. To put it another way, innovation is often a messy process. It should be no surprise that education ministries, which thrive on plans, order and predictability, find innovation so alien.

Innovation cannot be delivered, just in time, like a pizza from Domino's. However that does not mean the process of innovation cannot be managed and structured in a way that makes success more likely. Our high impact innovators share some important features in common. By understanding these features innovation could be made more manageable and the chances of success improved.

ABOVE: Tarsila Portella is responsible for Aprendiz's community learning and arts programmes; **LEFT:** Rich and poor live cheek by jowl in the centre of Sao Paulo. Aprendiz was created to bridge the gap

International flows of ideas have been a fertile source of inspiration. These schemes are not parochial. They thrive on international connections. Sometimes these connections are embodied in the careers of the founders. Take Sevda Bekman, one of the founders of MOCEP in Turkey, as an example. Bekman went to the American School in Istanbul where she met her best friend, Ayşen Özyeğin, who eventually became the project's main funder through her family's foundation. Bekman got involved in the MOCEP project after returning from doing a PhD at the Institute of Education in London. MOCEP itself is not a Turkish innovation: it was inspired by the Home Interaction Programme, first developed in Israel, which has since spread to several countries, most recently to Australia, where it was introduced in 2008.

Martin Burt went to the American school in Asunción before winning a scholarship to go to college in the United States. On his return, unable to find work under the then dictatorship because his family was blacklisted, Burt set up Fundación Paraguaya as the first organisation in Latin America to promote microcredit. Vicky Colbert, of Escuela Nueva, went to the American School in Bogotá, before studying in the United States and returning to Colombia to put into practice the novel educational thinking she had been exposed to. Rana Dajani started We Love Reading in Jordan after her children went to public libraries in the United States while she was studying. The Shafallah Center brings together international expertise from all over the world. Each of these innovations came from the reinterpretation of international ideas applied to a local context. Aprendiz exemplifies the process.

"According to Dewey, thinking and learning are stimulated when people are inspired to collaborate to solve a shared problem."

Aprendiz's international connections go even deeper than Gilberto Dimenstein's period studying in the United States. Aprendiz is one arm of an international movement to promote learning communities that was inspired by the Spanish educator César Coll and is centred on Barcelona, the capital of Catalonia. Coll was influenced by Latin American philosopher Paulo Freire's "liberation pedagogy" and the American philosopher of education, John Dewey, who argued education should unite thought and action. The two philosophers also had an impact on Vicky Colbert. According to Dewey, thinking and learning are stimulated when people are inspired to collaborate to solve a shared problem. Dewey criticised the way that schools taught subjects in isolation and argued instead for an education based on "constructive occupations" in real-world settings that would involve the student, mobilise their curiosity and sustain their interest.

Dewey's ideas took root in Spain in the 1930s, only to be extinguished under Franco's dictatorship. They were resuscitated when Spain became a democracy and fed Coll's movement. Around the same time Anisio Teixeira, a Brazilian educator, also felt Dewey's influence while he was studying at Columbia University, in New York. In the early 1950s Teixeira returned to Brazil to create the Carneiro Ribeiro Educational Centre, also known as the "park school", in the state of Bahia. Teixeira's project combined a "classroom school" and a "park school" which was dedicated to experiments and practical activities, for learning by doing. At that time Brazilian debates about learning were influenced by the radical French pedagogue Célestin Freinet, founder of the Modern School movement, who installed a printing press in his elementary school in Provence to allow his pupils to make their own newspapers. Freinet believed pupils should learn by making products and providing services; through collaborative, enquiry-based learning and trial and error; by a focus on the children's interests and natural curiosity as the starting point for learning; making learning authentic by using the real experiences that children had rather than abstract knowledge; encouraging children to take responsibility for their own work and for the school as a community. Aprendiz's learning neighbourhoods are an echo of Teixeira's park school and Coll's learning community. The project brings to communities throughout Brazil ideas that it has borrowed and adapted from France, Spain and the United States.

These international flows of ideas do not go just one way, north to south, rich to poor. A potent example of how the flow can go in reverse, taking an innovation from the developing world into the developed, is the Cristo Rey network developed by Jesuits in the United States.

Cristo Rey's mission is to provide children from poor, inner-city, usually ethnic minority households with a high quality, pre-college education that will get them into a decent university. Many of the public schools that serve such communities give children little hope of getting to college. Good private schools are beyond the means of households living on the breadline. The innovation at the heart of Cristo Rey is that each student works five or six days a month with a local employer. The school operates an employment agency; it makes sure the children turn up to work and that the job they do is properly paid and not exploitative. The rest of the school week is organised into four longer

FAR LEFT: A teacher at the Cristo Rey school, Boston; **NEAR LEFT:** Students prepare for a passing-out parade; **BELOW:** Scenes from student life at the Cristo Rey school, Boston

"Our mission begins where the roads run out."

school days to make time for children to go out to work. The children's earnings pay for their schooling. Not only do the children get a good education and better chance of making it to college, they learn while they work. In the process they build up an impressive CV – by the time they apply for college they should have done at least three years' work with reputable employers.

The idea of turning a school into an employment agency came, as many of these innovations did, from outside education: a management consultant, Rick Murray, who was brought in by the Jesuits to find a financial model to support their school. Murray got his idea by reflecting on his own education at the progressive Roeper School in Detroit which had been founded by German refugees George and Annemarie Roeper. The Roepers wanted to create a school for gifted children as a response to the horrors of Nazism. Murray spent three years with the Roepers in what he described as an "absolutely extraordinary learning community." One part of the education was "service internships" also known as "community duties." Murray worked as a teachers' aide, a carpenter, a bus supervisor and a stockbroker. Some of his most important learning, he realised, took place not in the classroom but when he was working. Murray's internships had been unpaid but they were the source for his idea that Cristo Rey could fund itself if the children got paid for working.

The inspiration for the Cristo Rey movement, however, came from Peru. Father John Foley, who set up the first Cristo Rey school in Chicago, had spent the previous thirty years in Peru. It was there that Foley met Jeff Thielman, who had spent three years working in Peru in the mid-1980s as a volunteer teacher. With the support of the Jesuits, Thielman set up the Cristo Rey Center for the Working Child in the city of Tacna. Foley took over that centre when Thielman returned to the United States. The centre offers working children a health centre, a legal aid clinic, an eight-classroom school with cafeteria, a library, a chapel and four rooms for technical training. Since its inception the centre has helped about 6,000 working children. It was Foley's work with this centre that drew him to the attention of senior Jesuits in Chicago when they were looking for someone to create a mould-breaking inner-city school. Once Foley got going he brought in Thielman as the founder director of the Cristo Rey school network. Thielman is now President of the Cristo Rey school in Boston.

Their shared experience in Peru gave Foley and Thielman insights into how to innovate in harsh conditions, insights that they could not have got in the United States. The Center for the Working Child could not afford to be precious about children working. Tacna's street kids had to work to put food in their mouths. The Centre had to provide them with an education that would fit alongside their work. When Foley and Thielman got back to the United States they inverted the idea they had developed in Peru: they found a way for children to work, alongside their school lessons. The same ingredients – work and learning – were blended in a different way. Next door to the Center for the Working Child in Tacna is a school that is part of the Fe y Alegría (Faith and Joy) movement created in the 1960s by Jesuit priest María Vélaz in Venezuela. Fe y Alegría is a primary and secondary educational programme for the poor that has grown into a movement with more than 12,000 schools and 1m children in programmes throughout Latin America. One of Fe y Alegría's slogans is: "Our mission begins where the roads run out." It focuses on the very poor by building schools where there are none. The single-minded clarity of Fe y Alegría's mission and its determination to build a mass movement directly inspired the Cristo Rey network which now encompasses 24 schools. Teams from Cristo Rey have visited Fe y Alegría to learn from their programme.

Cristo Rey started from a very particular place, Pilsen in downtown Chicago. But it brought to Pilsen ideas from a diverse range of sources, including Germany, Peru and Venezuela.

Our innovators act as a bridge, connecting and embedding ideas in the communities they serve. They work patiently with those communities to understand their needs and mobilise their support. They win local support because they need the resources and commitment that communities bring. Rewrite the Future was a global campaign yet according to Tove Wang it only worked because it gave communities a sense of ownership over education. "If people feel they own the school, that it's their school, they will protect it and look after it," she explained. Sugata Mitra's Hole in the Wall programme works because it bends to the way different communities want to use its computers. Norman Rowen and Carolyn Acker listened for hours to people on Regent Park before coming to any conclusions about what they needed. Yet these innovators are cosmopolitan rather than parochial. Outward-looking and curious, they bring to these places ideas that may have come from thousands of miles away.

"Since its inception the centre has helped about

6,000

working children."

Nor are our innovators precious about where they get ideas from. Innovators are inveterate borrowers. The best way to have a new idea is to mix together two existing ideas to create a new blend. Often this involves reworking old ideas rather than inventing something from scratch. The Weekend School in the Netherlands is a secular reworking of the religious Sunday school. There is nothing new in Latin America about farm schools. Martin Burt added a new twist to an old model. The idea behind the highly collaborative, interactive, project-based learning at the African Institute for Mathematics was inspired by Chris Engelbrecht's School of Physics, an annual summer programme started in the 1970s that brought an international faculty to Cape Town for three weeks to teach classes around their current research interests. Innovators are great at remixing existing ideas to make them more powerful and valuable. They are not afraid to delve into the past to retrieve ideas that have been discarded. Some of the best innovations are a potent mix of the very old and the very new.

Our pioneers are blenders in another sense: they combine principle with practicality. The principles behind their work often come from independent academic thinking about learning, which underlines the importance of rigorous academic research as one source of innovation. The Mother Child Education Program started life as an academic research programme. Sugata Mitra started his work from an academic base exploring an intellectual research question: could children teach themselves using computers? The IMC Weekend School grew out of Heleen Terwijn's research into depression in the Surinamese community in Amsterdam. But high-minded inquisitiveness needs to be married to making ideas work in practice. The Mother Child Education Program took off when the academics were matched to the business and managerial drive of Ayla Goksel, the chief executive with a background in banking. Carolyn Acker's inspirational vision for Regent Park only took shape when Norman Rowen patiently devised the detailed programme that became Pathways to Education. Vicky Colbert's ideas for Escuela Nueva took concrete form when she started working with skilled rural educators who had already devised something similar. Innovation and entrepreneurship rarely come from lone individuals. They almost always involve partnerships and teams that combine the different skills needed to turn an idea into a prototype and then to scale it.

Our pioneers are pragmatists with principles. Most of them come from outside the educational establishment. Indeed, time and again our innovators faced the greatest scepticism from the people who knew most about education.

Independent finance was as important for these new ventures as independent ideas and insights from outside education. Only Vicky Colbert in Colombia started from a base within an education ministry and even that was a rural outpost. MIT's OpenCourseWare programme and the TESSA initiative depended on their strong institutional bases for early funding. However most of the other programmes depended on funding from independent foundations to get going. Pathways to Education's early work was supported by a range of independent foundations. Cristo Rey was initially funded by the Catholic Church and a mixture of foundations. The network's expansion relied on funding from the Bill and Melinda Gates Foundation and the B.J. Cassin Foundation. The Citizens Foundation relies on contributions mainly from Pakistanis at home and abroad. Martin Burt was able to start his farm school with the profits from Fundación Paraguaya's microcredit programme. Foundations play a hugely significant role at the very earliest stages of innovation, funding models with huge potential that education ministries can be too clumsy, bureaucratic and risk-averse to support.

Finally, our pioneers are patient, persistent problem-solvers. They devise projects based on simple, compelling ideas that serve a clear need. Their projects do not require rocket science, even when they involve new technology. Their appeal can be summed up in a sentence: mothers can be trained to be educators (MOCEP); a neighbourhood can become a school (Aprendiz); children can learn by working and pay for their education in the process (Cristo Rey and Fundación Paraguaya); students can learn without having a teacher present so long as they have a good guide in the form of a book (Escuela Nueva), a computer programme (Hole in the Wall) or a lecture on video (MIT OpenCourseWare). Yet turning these simple ideas into effective programmes is often a protracted process that requires patience and determination. For Vicky Colbert at Escuela Nueva and Sevda Bekman at MOCEP, that process has taken 25 years. Change is frustratingly slow.

Innovation comes from many sources and in many forms. The kinds of innovation profiled in this book are just a small fraction of what is needed. Our innovators do not have all the answers. There is a mass of innovation within formal education systems that our sample does not represent. Policy-makers innovate by creating new financial models and incentives, such as vouchers and conditional cash payments, opening ways for new schools to be created. Practitioners innovate with new approaches to teaching, such as the phonics approach to literacy. Technology companies are creating new software and tools to be used in classrooms. This kind of innovation from within the system, designed to sustain and improve existing models, should not be underestimated. Yet our innovators shed light on where radical innovation in education comes from: innovation that will create new models of education that can work at scale, including for the very poorest and hardest to reach populations, often the people traditional systems fail most.

These pioneers provide several lessons about how innovation gets started and what would need to be done to generate more:

■ The search for innovation should not be confined to mainstream education systems. The most radical innovations may come from the most unlikely and marginal places.

■ Innovation will be fed by enabling the international flow and exchange of ideas, especially if those ideas can be taken up by people committed to applying them in a local context. Our pioneers are cosmopolitan in outlook but rooted in the communities they are serving. Creating bridges between communities that need innovation and international flows of ideas that can stimulate innovation would thus pay dividends.

■ Independent academic research into learning and child development was a source of inspiration for several of these projects. Academia is an important source of new thinking and fundamental ideas. Yet academic ideas need to be combined with practical programmes and people, to turn them into action. Funding promising academic research but also linking these programmes to practical problem-solving should produce more innovation.

■ Innovation programmes will be more successful if they attract talent from outside education, as well as inside, and are not afraid of confronting systems with a challenge.

■ Funding for radical educational innovation rarely comes from education ministries. There will be more innovation if more resources can be made available for early stage investment and if that funding can be invested wisely in the most promising projects.

The pioneers who have created these projects are blenders: they mix principle and pragmatism, the old and the new, the cosmopolitan with the community. They are often patient and persistent problem-solvers but deeply frustrated with how long it takes to change embedded systems. They have to be ambitious and confident to overcome sceptics and doubters,

yet also humble enough to borrow and listen when it makes sense. Above all they need endurance and a sense of mission, to survive a highly protracted process in which there are as many lows as highs. They believe in education but do not see themselves as educationalists. They are creative deviants. Few of them would be regarded as young. Age is almost entirely irrelevant in the make-up of innovators. Most are what might be called "grey-haired" revolutionaries. They do not wear hoodies and flip-flops, sit on beanbags and play with Lego, in the manner of Facebook and Google employees. They inspire teams of people with different skills to come together in a common cause. The people who create teams are often quite extraordinary people.

They have one other characteristic in common. As the white-haired Fritz Hahne put it, his bright eyes flashing wide, his face broken into a mischievous smile: "When Neil Turok came up with this idea a lot of people said 'great idea but it will never work'. When I heard about it I said 'great idea, we have to make it work'. But then I am a mad kind of guy." Aref Husseini, the founder of the Al-Nayzak project in Palestine, also fits that description. Husseini left a well-paid job as an engineer with Intel to start an NGO to encourage children to learn science in more imaginative and open ways, including an annual Palestine Science and Technology Fair which each year attracts 2,500 budding inventors to present their ideas in a competition to win a research grant. Husseini started as a travelling salesman, going from school to school teaching physics in unusual ways: "I was like Santa Claus with the bags, you know, travelling between the schools, a crazy, crazy man." Thousands of miles away in The Citizens Foundation's Karachi headquarters Mushtaq Chhapra said almost exactly the same thing: "We started with a goal of building 1,000 schools. People told us we were mad. But if you aren't mad you cannot do things in Pakistan. Thank God we had that streak of madness because to date we've built 730 schools."

Radical innovation starts in the most unlikely places. It also comes from people who may seem slightly crazed, especially to those who are schooled in traditional and conservative ways of doing things. Radical innovators have to put up with being thought slightly mad by people who claim to know better. Education will need more such people to generate more innovation. Generating innovation, creating a promising prototype or pilot, however, is just the first step. What stands out about our pioneers is that they have managed to take their ideas to scale, sometimes reaching millions of people. The next chapter explains the surprising and unusual ways they have achieved that.

A Shine project school,
Cape Town

CHAPTER 10

WE ARE A MOVEMENT

Young girls clamour for books at the end of a We Love Reading session in a mosque in Amman

Men are pouring out of the first-floor prayer room in the Bir al-Walidain mosque on a street corner in the neighbourhood of Al-Rabia, close to the centre of Amman, the Jordanian capital. At the mosque's side entrance there are unmistakable signs that something quite different is taking place on the floor below: a large pile of children's shoes is gathered by the door. Downstairs, in the corner of a large open room, about 30 young children, mostly aged five to eight, mainly girls, are gathered intently around a woman sitting on a chair. Their mothers sit along the wall or on the floor, legs outstretched. Everyone is attentively focused on the woman, waiting to see what she does. From a colourful bag by her side she pulls out a toy watermelon and describes a story she is going to read for them. The children sit enraptured. Then she hands out finger puppets, before leading them in a song about birds. A girl of eight is selected to read a story to the group. Then comes the highlight of the hour: the children are invited forward to take a book from a selection of about 60 the reader carries with her. Mayhem breaks out. There is a mad dash to be first in the queue. Some children are so determined to get the book they want, they jump the queue to open direct negotiations with the reader. The children know the books, the authors and even the names of the illustrators. After helping the reader sort out the books the mothers linger in a gaggle, chatting, laughing, sharing dates, wafers and coffee. The room is a women's space but it is also a space for reading, books and the imagination.

This little group was started by an Amman mother, Rola Abdel Hadi, after hearing on the radio about a scheme called We Love Reading that was training mothers to lead reading aloud to groups in mosques. Rola signed up and after two days' training recruited her first mothers by word of mouth and handing out leaflets in a local park. The group quickly reached its capacity. We Love Reading trained her to put drama, emotion and expression into her stories. It shows, according to one of the mothers staying behind: "The lady who reads aloud has made a unique environment in the mosque. The children wait day by day, hour by hour, to enjoy it, especially because they can then take the books home and read themselves."

This group in the Bir al-Walidain mosque is part of what is becoming a movement to promote a new culture of independent reading for pleasure in Jordan, and perhaps in time across the Middle East. The We Love Reading movement was started by a remarkable woman: Rana Dajani.

Dajani is Jordanian but she grew up in the United States, and eventually found herself with four children and studying a PhD in molecular biology at the University of Iowa: "I would spend all my time doing my research with my mice in the lab and my four children would spend all their time at the public library." They enjoyed a culture where reading was a pleasure. Yet when the family returned to Amman they found it very hard to keep up the habit. There were few libraries and even those that allowed in children were not keen to lend them books. So Dajani, as a diligent mother, started buying books to read to her children. Yet she became consumed by guilt that other children were not getting the same opportunity and as she was keen to make a larger contribution to her society, Dajani asked the local mosque whether she could set up a group where twice a month she would read to local children. The Imam announced the first session at Friday prayers in February 2006. Dajani was up and running, albeit slowly.

For three years she worked on her own. She would dress up in funny costumes, wear a special hat, read the children two or three books and then hand out others at the end of the session. Her house became known as the home of the *hakawati*, the story-teller. Eventually her work came to the attention of Synergos, a leading New York philanthropic non-profit, and in 2009 she won its Arab World Social Innovation prize. With that Dajani got both some money and a media profile that allowed her to take the next step and turn her personal project into an organisation: We Love Reading. "A lot of great innovations come from the individual and they never get carried on to the next stage, to the NGO, because they get lost. Like me. If I hadn't got this award I would still be reading in my neighbourhood but it wouldn't have spread or it would have taken a much longer time," she says.

We Love Reading is still a fledgling organisation, with just one full-time staff member as well as Dajani, who continues to be Professor of Molecular Biology at the Hashemite University. There are a few part-timers and a host of volunteers. We Love Reading trains mothers so they can set up their own read aloud group in their local mosque, for children aged 4–10. The mothers pay a nominal sum and Denise Assad, a Palestinian artist, trains them in storytelling techniques. They get a kit to start their group including a collection of about 30 different books for the children to take home each week. The kit sustains the group for about six months, by which time they can recruit more children to use the same books or buy more books to sustain the group. "They are children's books," Dajani says, "so the mothers do not need a university degree to be able to

LEFT MIDDLE: Rana Dajani, founder of We Love Reading, with a group in an Amman mosque; **ABOVE LEFT:** Amman in the evening sun; **ABOVE:** The still concentration of children at a We Love Reading group; **OTHER PICTURES:** We Love Reading in action

It is early days for We Love Reading but already it has trained about 420 people and about 100 groups have been set up, catering for perhaps

4,000 children

read them. They are well within their range." It is early days for We Love Reading but already it has trained about 420 people and about 100 groups have been set up, catering for perhaps 4,000 children. Yet Dajani has ambitions to take the scheme all over Jordan and perhaps beyond. She stands a good chance of succeeding because We Love Reading has the ingredients of what it takes to become a high impact innovator.

The key is not that she is a remarkable, entrepreneurial and charismatic leader. Nor is it essential that she create a highly professional organisation to take her idea forward. She needs a good organisation but not one that would pass muster with McKinsey consultants. We Love Reading already combines five elements that from the evidence of our pioneers seem critical to achieving impact at scale.

BELOW: Rana Dajani explains why she set up the We Love Reading programme; **RIGHT:** One of the books used in the programme

First, Dajani has developed a simple, effective product that appeals strongly to its market of mothers and children: a step-by-step guide to creating a read aloud group in your community. Dajani's training method is simple, useful, repeatable and reliable.

Second, she has turned a personal project, driven by her passion, into an organisation, with basic systems to sustain it: fundraising, grant application writing, delivering training programmes. This is the first step to scaling up.

Third, We Love Reading depends on networks. Many organisations, both commercial and social, mistake their own growth – in sales, revenues, profits, members – for success. The bigger the organisation gets the more successful it must be. We Love Reading measures its success by how many children it gets involved in reading groups. To achieve that it needs to connect three networks: a network of funders, who will provide the money; the mothers who set up and run the local groups; the mosques that will provide the space for the groups to meet. This is a frugal model because it relies on self-help and it piggybacks on the infrastructure that mosques already provide, as Dajani explains: "They have the space, it's safe, it's got a carpet, it's got a bathroom. I mean, it's perfect. You don't have to build it, it's just sitting there." High impact innovators achieve scale usually by drawing on networks that already exist and piggybacking on existing infrastructures.

Fourth, the women are becoming more than a network. They are already starting to resemble a movement to bring about social change through reading, albeit a movement that operates without attracting much attention, making much noise or seeking confrontation. We Love Reading could be renamed the Mothers Reading Aloud Movement, with the aim of bringing about long-term cultural change.

We Love Reading is not delivering a service, which it needs to support with a complex supply chain; it is creating a capability in hundreds upon hundreds of local women, enabling them to do something creative for themselves. "It's not just a reading project, you are changing a woman, you are giving her a lot of tools and a lot of confidence to do something on

her own and it's not too much of a push because she is still in the neighbourhood."

Fifth, organisations need hierarchies, but movements need causes, shared values, common goals and even enemies to pull them together and give them a purpose. That is the final ingredient, which Dajani has to provide: a common cause. For Dajani reading is the means, but her cause is to get children at a young age to realise they can and should think for themselves.

We Love Reading is several things at once. It is a method for training mothers to create reading groups. It is an organisation that supports that method. The organisation, however, is the junction box for a network of funders, women and mosques. The women are becoming akin to a movement for reading, which is animated by a common cause, opening the imagination of children so they can think for themselves. Dajani needs to innovate across all five of these areas at the same time – method, organisation, network, movement and cause – to be successful. That is the recipe almost all the other innovators have deployed to generate their impact.

In *Forces for Good* Leslie Crutchfield and Heather McLeod Grant set out to uncover how twelve of the most successful social ventures in the United States achieved their impact. They found that success did not stem from superior management, better organisation nor even from access to more resources, but from these organisations' ability to mobilise wider networks around common goals. Instead of growing their own organisation, site by site, to achieve high impact, the successful organisations achieved large impact while remaining relatively small themselves. They pulled off this trick by constantly looking to mobilise members, inspire followers, encourage emulators, create networks, seed movements, shape government policy and recruit evangelists. As a result, often small organisations had a big impact thanks to the way they leveraged social movement and networks. Crutchfield and McLeod Grant put it this way: "The secret to success lies in how great organisations mobilise every sector of society – government, business, non-profits and the public – to be a force for good. In other words, greatness has more to do with how non-profits work outside the boundaries of their organisations than how they manage their own internal operations… They work with and through others to create more impact than they could ever achieve alone."

Our high impact innovators follow a version of the approach that Crutchfield and McLeod Grant found in the United States. To put it in a nutshell they see themselves as building not just organisations, but movements. There are five elements to this approach. All are essential to success; none is sufficient on its own.

SERVICES AND METHODS ▪▪▪ Innovation counts for little unless it produces something tangible that people can use, a product or methods that make them more productive or which help to solve a problem. Our innovators have all created reliable, repeatable methods, processes, services or tools which people can use to learn more effectively. These methods are akin to the organisation's signature. Escuela Nueva's signature is in its learning guides, which allow children to learn independently and collaboratively. TESSA's signature is its highly adaptable modules that can be applied in a range of countries so teachers can learn new techniques. MIT created an entirely new practice for learning: following courses online, through video lectures with accompanying notes. The kernel of these projects is a simple innovation that successfully meets a clear need. That is the basis for their credibility.

ORGANISATIONS ▪▪▪ Innovation rarely gets beyond first base when it relies on a charismatic teacher, parent or entrepreneur. The first step to scale is to create an organisation, which will turn the initial innovation, often deeply embedded in context, into a scaleable product that people can apply in other settings. Carolyn Acker and Norman Rowen turned their painstaking homegrown innovation into a Pathways to Education programme that could be used across Canada. The Citizens Foundation has a highly effective organisation to raise funds and build new schools.

NETWORKS ▪▪▪ These organisations, however, are designed to mobilise existing networks rather than trying to deliver everything themselves. They turn their weakness, their lack of resources, into a strength, by mobilising the resources of other organisations. Nanhi Kali is built on a partnership between two foundations and works through scores of NGOs and hundreds of schools. TESSA is built on a network that links the Open University in the United Kingdom to 18 institutions of higher and further education across Africa. They multiply their impact by working with and through other organisations rather than trying to do it all themselves.

MOVEMENTS ▬▬Time and again our innovators told us they were leading a movement not just an organisation. They want to create large communities animated by a shared purpose. They set out to inspire followers and they welcome emulators. Alumni play a vital role in this. Schools are like production lines: once one batch of students leaves, another replaces it. Our innovators create communities to which alumni continue to contribute long after they have left the programme. That is how the African Institute of Mathematical Sciences will multiply its impact. Neil Turok and Fritz Hahne hope to create a network of AIMS centres that will produce 750 graduates a year. Those graduates will go on to play key roles in their societies, providing not just skills but spreading the culture that AIMS promotes. These are organisations designed to build movements.

CAUSES ▬▬ A movement needs a cause to which people can pledge their allegiance. Our innovators have to excel in articulating a compelling moral mission as well as getting things done. Rewrite the Future built its campaign by shaming governments into making good on their promises to children in zones of conflict. The Citizens Foundation and Cristo Rey are built on the cause of bringing good quality education to the poorest children. The OpenCourseWare programme garnered support from academics at MIT because it fitted so well with the university's mission to share knowledge. The Shafallah Center's mission is to show that all children, including those with a disability, can have a decent education.

There is nothing new in this. Some of the most successful brands, and especially those that appeal to young people, clothe their products in values to make them more appealing. Nike became successful when it began to associate its products, through advertising and marketing, with individual willpower, determination and social mobility. Apple makes great products but much of its appeal comes from the way its cool design embodies its values: rip, mix, burn.

Yet often innovators have to be prepared to go even further: to challenge orthodoxy, especially at points where it is most vulnerable to challenge. Sugata Mitra's Hole in the Wall programme is at its most effective where the traditional system breaks down and cannot provide good quality teachers. That is where his alternative ideology of self-organised learning makes most sense. Innovators in education, if they become successful, quickly find that they are confronted with opposition from entrenched professional ideologies about education. They have to be skilled at picking their fights, building up a

coalition of support for their approaches, while also winning converts away from more traditional methods. That is why these innovators are careful to show that they improve students' chances of doing well in traditional terms: completing their grades, getting through exams, following the curriculum and making it to college. They deploy novel methods to achieve these ends and they aim to provide a more enriching and imaginative education. Yet they guard their backs and maintain their legitimacy by doing a good job in traditional terms – getting children their grades.

High impact social innovators do not get off first base unless they have an effective, reliable product that meets an important need: learning to read; supporting girls at school; making available online a mass of courses that were previously unavailable; getting children into college. To get beyond first base they have to create an organisation that is capable of attracting the resources to replicate what they do in several places, thus establishing its credibility and showing the same approach can work in different settings. At that point these high impact innovators do not, however, tend to continue to scale their own organisation to roll out more of their own programmes. Instead they multiply their impact by working with and though a network of other organisations, mobilising supporters and followers. This is the route to high social impact, at affordable cost: piggybacking on the resources of other organisations and turning the commitment of followers into voluntary effort and community self-help. None of that is possible unless the project articulates a clear, compelling cause, which gives people something to believe in and work for. Our pioneers build movements not just organisations.

The story of how they attain high-scale impact does not, however, end there. The final instalment is what happens when movements come face to face with bureaucratic, hierarchical, government education systems.

ABOVE RIGHT: Academic Support Centre for primary students at NM Joshi Municipal School, Delisle Road, near Bawla Masjiid, Curry Road (w), Mumbai. While primarily girls, a small number of boys are allowed to attend if they need, although they are not registered to the Nanhi Kali programme; RIGHT: Classroom for Nanhi Kali academic support to secondary students in Sitaram Mill Compound School, near NM Joshi Marg, Police Station, Lower Parel, Mumbai

"Our pioneers build movements not just organisations."

Drawing done by the daughter
of Rana Dajani, pioneer
of We love Reading, Amman,
Jordan

THE CLASH: WHEN MOVEMENTS MEET SYSTEMS

Young boys such as these on the streets of Mumbai have been the beneficiaries of a massive expansion of access to schooling

Vicky Colbert gives a shrug of her shoulders and opens the palms of her hands in a show of resignation: "It is very difficult to get success at scale without government backing, but it is very difficult to do it with government as well." Colbert is slightly unusual: she is the only innovator in our group who started her work within the Ministry of Education, albeit a distant outpost in rural Colombia. Over the years she has become a veteran of working the corridors of power in Bogotá. The experience has taught her to be cautious about handing over innovations to the state: "Government gives you scale but the cost is quality. Innovation tends to fade away inside a bureaucracy. You lose fidelity to the model. Once you give the state your baby, your innovation, you cannot be sure what is going to happen to it."

That sentiment is widely shared among our innovators. Martin Burt put it this way: "More investment in education does not necessarily mean more learning, because so much of the money gets lost in bureaucracy. We want to influence and shape government thinking and policy but we don't want to take government money because it comes with so many strings." Mushtaq Chhapra is troubled by the same dilemma as he looks to the future of The Citizens Foundation: "The government in Pakistan recognizes that The Citizens Foundation needs to be taken seriously but we don't want government interference in our system. Once we get into that it becomes very difficult. I feel that unless and until The Citizens Foundation can influ-ence the government system, the big issues will not be addressed. We show the way forward for the government but we are The Citizens Foundation, we are not a state."

In seeking to scale their innovations beyond the networks and movements that they create, our innovators face a seemingly intractable dilemma: they cannot do it without the state but they find it incredibly hard to do it with the state.

Government has played the critical role in scaling mass schooling by: legislating to mandate children's attendance at school; funding and building schools; training and employing teachers in their millions; setting exams and regulating the quality of schools. Education systems that started with social entrepreneurs and religious societies have been endorsed, controlled and expanded by governments. Creating education systems was part of a programme for national unification and modernisation in the nineteenth century.

In the United Kingdom in the 1830s it was easy for a reasonably literate man to set up a school in his front room and attract fee-paying pupils. Unmarried women set up "dame schools" in their homes and gardens. Most elementary education was unregulated. The roots of the modern British school system lie in Sunday schools which taught reading to promote Bible study. By the mid-nineteenth century the Newcastle Commission found that schooling was the norm for most of the young in England. The Elementary Education Act of 1870 redefined schooling as a compulsory, age-specific, professional teacher-directed, school-based exercise aimed at the mastery of prescribed school subjects grouped around a central core of basic literacy. Most of Europe trod the same path, inspired and frightened in equal measure by the links between Prussian military success and its regimented school system. By 1900 compulsory elementary education was established in most of western Europe (Belgium, the laggard, followed suit in 1920). In Europe the proportion of children attending school went from about 25% in 1870 to 75% in 1900.

The United States started the nineteenth century with children being educated in church basements, private houses and one-room rural schoolhouses. By 1850 all US states had government-funded primary education but only 50% of American children attended school. By 1900 all states required attendance at elementary school and about 10% of

Helena Singer, from Aprendiz
in Brazil

14–17 year olds went to high school. By 1980 nine in ten attended high school and 70% graduated. Schools became larger, more complex and systematised. Between 1930 and 1980 the number of high schools in the United States barely changed but the number of students enrolled rose from 592,000 to 2,743,000. The number of days students spent at school rose from 99 in 1900 to almost 160 in 1958. Spending per pupil tripled between 1920 and 1950.

In 1850 most education in Europe and the United States was provided by private, voluntary and church groups, in loosely regulated schools that relied on independent funding. A century later most children were attending publicly funded schools that were more specialised, complex and sophisticated institutions. Education had become system-funded and regulated by government. Modern education started life with innovators in church basements and private homes. It became a mass activity involving millions of children thanks to the way governments mobilised resources to make that possible. That recipe might first have been developed in the US and Europe but it is now being followed across the world. The numbers explain why.

When The Citizens Foundation reaches its goal of building 1,000 schools in Pakistan it will be a remarkable achievement. But that will be only 0.5% of schools in the country. To reach millions of children TCF will probably have to work with the government to change how the public education system operates. The Mother Child Education Program has reached about 300,000 mothers in Turkey: no mean feat. But by getting the Turkish government to endorse its programme it will reach 20 million mothers, according to Ayla Goksel. Escuela Nueva's methods are used in 17,000 Colombian primary schools only because the government adopted the programme. The Vietnamese government recently mandated all rural primary schools to use the Escuela Nueva approach, at a stroke reaching many millions of children. Any other route to scale would have taken decades. Our innovators want to maximise their impact. That is why most accept they have to work with government.

There are good reasons why government, for its part, should be interested in innovative projects that start in civil society: they represent free research and development for systems that are heavily focused on day-to-day operations. All public systems need a flow of new ideas to adapt to emerging needs, exploit new technologies and to find better solutions to problems. Policy-makers have begun to recognise that government systems need to open up. In the United States, Charter

Schools receiving public money yet not subject to all government regulations, have played a vital if controversial role in creating new educational opportunities (although only about a quarter are clearly a success). In England the government has created openings for parents and companies to form and sponsor new schools. In Sweden parents can claim funding from the state to create independent schools. One of the most impressive school networks in the world is the Kunskapsskolan group, which offers highly personalised but very methodical to approaches to learning that allow students to set their own targets and learn at their own pace. It was started by a group of Swedish companies, outsiders to education.

School systems are rich in resources but often in need of new ideas to improve their performance. Social innovators are rich in ideas but in need of resources to scale them up. Each should see the case for working with the other. The reality, however, is that too often they find themselves at odds.

Social innovators complain that government systems are slow-moving, bureaucratic, and risk-averse. Even when new ideas are endorsed and officially adopted they are often killed off in practice because they are starved of funds, watered down and rejected in practice by professionals. Teachers are often hostile to innovation that threatens to make their jobs more complicated. Teachers take up innovations that allow them to do their traditional jobs more effectively. That helps to explain why technologies that once promised to change classroom teaching – radio, television, video, computers – have been incorporated into traditional practices.

Teachers tell a different story. Often teachers claim to be ready to adopt innovative approaches but find their hands tied by a centralised curriculum, regular assessments and punitive inspections. Evidence of that comes from Pratham, the Indian educational non-profit, which ran summer schools so children at risk of falling behind could catch up. The summer schools produced outstanding results because the teachers, who came from normal public schools, employed imaginative and engaging techniques. Yet when Pratham contacted the same teachers back at work in government schools, they complained they could not teach the Pratham way because the curriculum would not allow it. Teachers are not alone in being wary of innovation. Parents can also be cautious about their children being subjected to wild educational experiments.

In Europe the proportion of children attending school went from about 25% in 1870 to

75% in 1900.

"literacy scores rose from 54% to 64% and graduation rates by 7% to **75%.**"

In their defence, policy-makers and politicians, responsible for very large school systems serving millions of children, complain that they need proven ideas they can rely upon. They cannot afford to take time experimenting with potentially interesting but untested ideas when parents, politicians and employers are clamouring for better results. When Ben Levin became the top government official in the education system of the state of Ontario in Canada he became responsible for a system with 5,000 schools serving 2m children. Levin wanted to improve performance across the board, for all children, in all schools. He did not have time to waste. His fascinating account, *How to Change 5000 Schools,* tells the story of a relentless effort to raise standards, by improving teaching and strengthening school leadership to focus on a few stretching targets: improving literacy and numeracy across 4,000 elementary schools and graduation rates from 800 high schools. Levin's strategy succeeded: literacy scores rose from 54% to 64% and graduation rates by 7% to 75%. Change on this scale needs a concerted strategy; it cannot be left to chance. For policy-makers like Levin the chief task is to drive incremental improvements in performance from the system as it stands. They are not that interested in creating something new unless it clearly serves that goal.

Many of these strategies for system-wide change trace their roots to the ideas of Michael Fullan, professor emeritus at the Ontario Institute for Studies in Education at the University of Toronto. Fullan worked with Sir Michael Barber, the architect of the British government's literacy and numeracy strategy in the late 1990s. Barber and Fullan recommend focussing relentlessly on how to improve teaching to hit a small number of measurable targets. Both stress the importance of building the collective capacity, motivation and will of teachers to change. However in practice the people on the receiving end often experience these strategies as centralised, mechanistic, and narrowly-focused. They leave little room for local initiative and reward compliance with formats handed down from on high. They often seem to be designed to change teachers' behaviour, without bothering to win their commitment. As Fullan puts it: "Local decision-makers and schools do not need to be empowered. They need to be engaged. There is lots of evidence that decentralisation will not yield improvements."

Our innovators see themselves as mobilising social movements. These policy-makers see themselves as engineering new systems. Formal systems and social movements do not mix well. Vicky Colbert says that Escuela Nueva "drifted" as it scaled up in the 1990s because there was no way to ensure the method was adopted in the right way by schools. The Mother Child Education Program started life as a two-year programme, became a 25-week programme as it was scaled up but has been adopted by the government as a 14-week programme, which teachers implement in their spare time. Rana Dajani, the founder of We Love Reading, can already see the conflict between bottom-up, organic social movements and top-down, explicit systems, looming on the horizon: "If the government would take this model and implement it, whoa! First the government would solve its people's problems very easily…it's efficient and it's sustainable and if the government implements it I do not have to go around recruiting women. On the other hand maybe you do really need to go through the other way to get the people involved. I don't like top-down initiatives. I like bottom-up. I think this builds confidence on the personal level and also builds independence that people do not depend on the government. In theory it's nice if the government could adopt but maybe the more difficult way is the better way in the long run because it's building the individual."

None of our innovators would claim to have a complete answer to this dilemma, but many have found ways to make the relationship between government and civil society, systems and movements, work better.

Some have become niche **providers** of a service to the larger system. They solve a problem that is difficult to fix from inside the system. Pathways to Education works alongside the school system, supporting children who find it particularly difficult to sustain their secondary education. Nanhi Kali does much the same for the poorest girls in schools in India. The Shine programme provides a module of literacy support within schools to help children keep up. These programmes are akin to external component suppliers to a larger product.

As well as providing services many of these organisations **advocate** changes to government policy and lead public debate on education. One model for this mix is Pratham, in India. As well as supporting millions of children at risk to stay in school, Pratham produces a highly influential annual survey on the quality of government education. Pratham delivers services *and* seeks to shape government policy. Its role as an advocate is underpinned by its reputation as an effective service provider. One of the most powerful examples of the combination of service and advocacy was Rewrite the Future. Its campaign persuaded aid donors to pledge $450m extra to provide better schools in conflict zones for about 10m children. It advocated change on the basis of its track record in delivering on the ground. A third approach is that of **programmers**: they infiltrate the system, like a virus, to reprogramme it with a new operating system. The prime example is Escuela Nueva: it is providing schools across Latin America with a new operating manual. This strategy often presents innovators with the most intense dilemmas: government endorsement offers to take their programmes to scale but also wrests control away from the originators, making it hard for them to maintain quality.

Inspirers avoid this dilemma by maintaining their independence. Inspirers provide a set of principles that emulators can follow. They do not try to grow their own organisation. The Shafallah Center in Doha is an inspirer: it has created a model for the education of disabled children that is being followed all over the world. The most impressive inspirer in our sample is MIT. MIT's decision to make its courses available for free online inspired a worldwide movement of universities that have followed suit, creating an entirely new way to distribute content.

Other projects have become **partners** with the system: they draw on the resources of the system but remain semi-detached. The African Institute of Mathematical Sciences was established as a joint venture between several universities and it only works because university lecturers from all over the world come to AIMS to deliver its courses. Students come to AIMS from African universities and they are on their way to further study at other universities. AIMS is like a junction-box connecting these universities. Barry Green its director is clear, however, that it could not exist if it were part of a university; it needs to be independent to maintain its own, free-flowing and collaborative culture. The Citizens Foundation is exploring how it could partner with the Pakistan government to take over the running of perhaps several thousands of public schools.

A final approach is pursued by a group of separatists who want to create a parallel but separate infrastructure alongside the government system. Martin Burt wants to create farm schools that pay for themselves to avoid having to be dependent on unreliable state funding. A few years ago it might have been easy to dismiss the separatists because it was so costly to create a large infrastructure for learning outside government. Two developments are changing all that.

The first is the spread of low-cost communications technologies and platforms, like YouTube and smartphones, which are creating opportunities for entrepreneurs to create new mass platforms for learning. A prime example is the explosive growth on YouTube of the Khan Academy, which has a storehouse of 2,400 videos, teaching everything from maths to physics. Khan's lessons have been seen more than 69m times. One of the big opportunities of the future will be to create large digital platforms for learning which people can easily add to and draw down from, and which support large communities of students and educators. Some of the largest multi-player computer games support communities of many millions. There is no reason why something similar should not be possible in education.

The second development is the extraordinary growth in many developing countries of low-cost private education aimed at relatively poor people, which has been extensively researched and advocated by James Tooley, the academic turned entrepreneur. In the developed world private schooling is for the rich. In the developing world it is increasingly a way for poor parents to escape dysfunctional state systems. In the shanty town of Makoko in Lagos, to take one example, Tooley found 32 unrecognised and unregulated private schools, deep in vast slums, where no government official would go. Private schools, Tooley says, are frugal innovators: they do not pay their teachers much; they set up in local houses, teach in local languages and attract a lot of self-help from parents. The growth of low-cost private schools, and private tutoring outside school hours, is driven by dissatisfaction with poorly performing government systems and the availability of young educated women who see in teaching a chance to have a career. Geeta Gandhi Kingdon, an Oxford University expert on education in the developing world, estimates that 96% of the increased enrolments in Indian primary schools between 1993 and 2000 were in often ramshackle private schools. Tooley's ideas are controversial with educationalists who see private education as pernicious and divisive. Yet so long as bureaucratic and highly unionised government systems remain impervious to reform and unable to meet the aspirations parents have for their children, the private sector is only likely to grow.

Innovators are finding a variety of ways to work with formal education systems. It is not easy but nor is it impossible. A larger, more fertile common ground needs to be created lying between government systems and civil society innovators.

Indeed system thinkers are moving in this direction, recognising that innovation is often as much about creating alliances and coalitions for change, as it is about reengineering.

Ben Levin says motivating teachers was at the heart of Ontario's improvement strategy, exciting in them a sense of moral purpose and self-confidence. Schools need to mobilise resources in their communities, parents and businesses, to help them. In short, according to Levin, improving a school system turns on leading a coalition of politicians, parents, teachers and pupils in a collective effort at change. Michael Fullan stresses the importance of teachers collaborating and being animated by a cause, seeing them almost as a movement: "It doesn't matter how much money you invest. You won't get results unless teachers are onside." Sir Michael Barber recently noted that the very best school systems rely more on a culture of self-motivation and improvement that is generated from within, rather than pushing from the centre. Tony Bryk and his colleagues came to much the same conclusion in *Organizing Schools for Improvement,* a study of the differences between 100 Chicago schools that improved and 100 that stagnated. The schools that improved had "student-centric" approaches to learning and leaders who saw it as their job to encourage professional teachers to focus on how to raise achievement while also forging stronger links between schools, families and local communities. Successful schools are like local movements. The best way to improve a system, in the long run, is to see it as a movement in the making, a coalition animated by a common cause.

Finding common ground between systems and movements is going to be vital to scale innovations that start outside the state system. Governments in much of the developing world are too stretched, the needs of their populations too deep, urgent and diverse, for them to go it alone. They need a strong civil society sector of innovators to work with them, providing new solutions, filling gaps, working with excluded groups, adapting new technologies. Success in the future will depend on government systems and social movements being brought together. Creating that common ground will be central to successful innovation strategies.

The campus of Qatar Foundation in Doha, which launched WISE

Detail from a school
in Bimasvaram

CHAPTER 12

OPENING THE DOOR TO INFINITY

The view towards Bogotá from a house ruined by annual floods and mudslides in the La Capilla favela

On this journey from Pakistan to Paraguay, Bogotá to Kampala, what have we learned about the state of innovation in education and how it can be strengthened? The answer to that question turns on three other questions that organise our conclusions.

First, how great is the need for innovation in education?

72 million

children are not enrolled in primary school, many of them in zones of conflict.

More children than ever are enrolled in schools that are reaching further than ever, into remote rural villages and into urban slums. The number of children not in school has fallen markedly in the last decade. Yet even so, significant challenges remain: 72m children are not enrolled in primary school, many of them in zones of conflict. Access to secondary school is more uneven. Overcoming the obstacles that stand in the way of these children getting to school – poverty, conflict, distance, discrimination – will require more ingenuity as well as investment, to provide accelerated learning to those who have been left out; delivering learning, perhaps digitally, in places that are not schools in communities that cannot afford them; employing more women teachers to make it easier for girls to persuade their parents to let them go to school. Rewrite the Future had to deploy many such innovations to get 10m children in conflict zones into better schools.

Yet just getting more children enrolled in school will not be enough. Too many children are enrolled in school but do not attend. Too many of those that do attend learn far too little. They fall behind, drop out and start to fail long before they reach the final hurdle. Too many children arrive at school full of hope only to find themselves in very large classes where they are subjected to rote learning in which they chorus answers to prompts from a teacher who drills them in routines they barely understand. Improving the quality of learning critically depends on more, better-trained, motivated and managed teachers who turn up every day and do their job well. That means professionals who are skilled at making learning engaging, meaningful and enjoyable. That is why innovations such as the TESSA programme count, providing low-cost tools for in-service teacher training so teachers can develop more innovative techniques. Escuela Nueva's learning guides make potentially chaotic multi-grade rural schools manageable and creative places to learn in. Complementary innovations, to provide children with high-quality opportunities to learn before and after they go to school, are also vital. That is what

Sugata Mitra's Hole in the Wall scheme did for children in the Madangir slum: the learning games on his computers supplemented the meagre diet they got at school. Heleen Terwijn's Weekend School does something similar for children in the Netherlands: providing an exciting Sunday supplement to their lessons in school.

So simply widening access to higher quality learning opportunities for all children will require lots more innovation. But there is a deeper, more structural problem: the growing misalignment between the kind of education that society needs and the education that our systems deliver.

For much of the twentieth century, in the industrialised world, there seemed to be a good fit between education systems and society. Education reflected the division of labour employed in large bureaucratic organisations: a system of grades, lessons, years and exams, all intricately timetabled. Work and education meant being able to follow instructions and respond in the right way, at the right time. It was factory-era schooling for a society dominated by factory models of organisation. Education systems, however, did not just serve an economic purpose. Reasonably uniform, national educational provision was one way that states unified disparate ethnic groups around common language, knowledge, codes, exams, holidays and rites of passage, such as going to and leaving school. Formal education systems were a vital tool in Europe and the United States to integrate and assimilate people into a common culture. Industrialised nation states in the nineteenth and twentieth centuries created the education systems they needed to be successful. These enormous, collective social innovations changed people's lives en masse mainly for the better: in 1850 in the United States or Britain it would have been unusual for a child from a working class home to study till the age of 16; in 1950 it was commonplace. For much of the twentieth century there seemed to be no need for innovation and little scope for it.

This has all changed, quite fundamentally, in the last few decades and it will continue to change in the decades to come.

The education systems we have do not do the job they were designed for well enough: the clearest evidence of that malfunction comes from the United States where large investments in education have yielded precious little by way of improved outcomes. The deeper problem is that the education systems we have inherited are increasingly out of kilter with the world our children will face as adults. The skills needed to prosper in the modern economy may well include a mastery of English and maths, computers and basic science, but they will also involve the ability to think critically, respond creatively, work with collaborators, act entrepreneurially, understand different cultures and viewpoints. Education systems need to encourage children to be protagonists not just recipients. Systems designed to integrate nation states are preparing children for a world of global flows and interconnections. Lessons organised for an era of books, newspapers and encyclopedias are being taken by children who already use Google, YouTube and Wikipedia. The gap between the systems we have and the systems we need is only going to grow.

We also find ourselves in a different position, because new means are becoming available for people to learn in new ways, principally through the Web and social media, smartphones and tablet computers, Google and immersive computer games. The video lecture could be the textbook of the future. The social network might provide the classmates. Games structured as learning guides could become lessons. These unfolding technology platforms have global reach at relatively low-cost and yet provide opportunities for deeply personalised and highly collaborative learning experiences which engage children as contributors and creators.

So we can look forward to an increasingly uncomfortable misfit between what education is, what it needs to become and what it could be. For most of the twentieth century there was neither much apparent need, nor much scope for innovation. In the twenty-first century both the need and scope for innovation should be ample.

The second question, which flows from this, is: are education systems well able to close the innovation gap, by delivering a flow of new ideas, methods, tools, teaching techniques and organisational models for learning? That inevitably raises issues about the kinds of innovation that are needed, what students should learn and how. The issue is not just how much innovation is needed but whether it is of the right kind and what it is designed to achieve. The huge debate over those issues will not be settled here. Putting those disputes to one side, however, a couple of things are clear about the kind of innovation education systems *are* good at.

Globally education is a huge industry, with an annual turnover of several trillion US dollars, supporting an infrastructure with a near global reach. These systems employ millions of skilled, trained professionals and those practitioners draw on the accumulated knowledge of academics and specialists in

universities and teacher training colleges. Education also has committed customers who want its product: even the poorest, least-educated parents will usually go to great lengths to get their children a basic education. Few industries can count on such customer loyalty. Examples of outstanding and innovative practice can be found all around the world, from methods for teaching maths, to new model schools and entire education systems, such as those in Finland, Ontario and Singapore. There is a growing international traffic in good ideas and best practices, fed by the appetite among educators, parents, policy-makers and politicians for better results. New players are deploying new technologies for learning, from Apple and Google to more established innovators such as the Open University and the BBC. Experiments with digital, distance and collaborative online learning are underway in scores of countries. Learners, not content to wait, are taking matters into their own hands, turning to the Khan Academy, YouTube, iTunes U and the burgeoning OpenCourseWare movement for learning guides. Policy-makers have begun to recognise the need to accelerate innovation, in part by opening the way for new entrants to bring in new ideas to challenge sometimes complacent systems. Every day in millions of schools and classrooms, on the Web and at home, people are devising new and more effective ways to learn, without ever asking permission nor seeking recognition. So far, so good.

Yet most of this monumental, collective effort at innovation is designed to improve existing models of education incrementally. These systems, moreover, are notoriously difficult to reform. They tend to be: risk-averse; inward-looking; prone to being dominated by producers, by teachers and their unions; resistant to decommissioning outdated approaches that are performing poorly. Incremental innovation from within the system does not go far enough or fast enough to close the gap between the education systems we have and those that we need, especially to meet the rapidly rising expectations of fast-growing societies in the developing world – India, Pakistan, Brazil, South Africa, Indonesia – which can ill afford to disappoint vast, young populations hungry for a better future. These young people are growing up in a culture which breeds higher expectations.

The spread of wi-fi and smartphones is creating a universal expectation that people should be able to connect to "the network" wherever they are. In the developing world the acquisition of a mobile phone has become a vital rite of passage: once you have a mobile you count. Facebook and social media are creating the expectation that you will be able to link to people, to find friends and collaborators. Wikipedia and the open educational resources movement is creating the universal expectation that knowledge should be available to all. Google has created the expectation that if a piece of information exists it should be discoverable. YouTube and mobile phones with cameras are creating the expectation that if something has happened we should be able to see it. Twitter has created the expectation that if something is happening we should be able to hear about it first hand, from people close to the real events. Blogging, feedback services and collaborative rating have created an expectation that we should be able to give our assessment of virtually any experience. The web and social media are creating a kind of civic long tail, a mass of loosely connected, small-scale conversations, around content that people expect to be able to enjoy, share, engage with and discuss. All systems, public and private, will have to contend with young people armed with these new expectations of how they should be treated. Education is not alone in finding this deeply challenging.

What education systems lack, and society needs, are more systematic ways to promote more radical forms of innovation, to create new models of learning that go beyond and challenge orthodox schooling. That will mean: new kinds of schools and educational institutions, like Escuela Nueva and the African Institute of Mathematical Sciences, which allow far more collaborative and participative learning; new ways for schools to work in tandem with exciting opportunities for children to learn in communities, as they do at Aprendiz and the

Weekend School; new platforms for people to learn entirely outside the traditional educational system, in informal settings, perhaps without the help of traditional teachers, using technologies like the Hole in the Wall and open courseware. These are no more than signals as to the kinds of change that are needed at much greater scale.

Education systems find it difficult to promote radical innovation, in part because that kind of innovation will often come from outside the mainstream. At least that is our judgement, based on a small and partial sample. To ground these judgements more securely, raise awareness and build consensus about the need for innovation, more research is needed. A first step would be systematically to compare education with comparable global industries which serve basic human needs – health, water, energy, food, communications – to compare how these other industries generate ideas, select the most promising, develop them into products and take them to scale. Certainly other industries have much more developed approaches to innovation. Retailers have sophisticated ways to understand their customers and manage brands. High technology industries rely on a flow of ideas from universities and venture capital-backed start-ups. Drug companies spend huge sums on basic research. In contrast education, as a global industry on a similar scale, seems to lack systematic and powerful ways to generate new models and take them to scale. Of course going into school is not like going to a supermarket: learning cannot be bought off the shelf. Yet that does not mean education could not learn from these comparisons.

Pictures of India's past political leaders underline the importance attached to education, in rhetoric if not reality, after independence in 1947

That leads to our final question: what should be the main ingredients of a more effective approach to promote more radical innovation?

An adequate answer would require another book but we think the following ingredients could be essential:

■ International flows of ideas are vital to feed innovation. Increasing the range and the depth of these exchanges, both face-to-face and online, should raise the rate of innovation. The more ideas there are in play, the more connections there are; the more new blends that are created, the more likely that some will be a success.

■ As well as learning from the best, and often the best-resourced schools – such as the high-tech Thomas Jefferson High School for Science and Technology in Alexandria, Virginia – more direct investment is needed in creating frugal, large-scale, simple, effective models that are designed for the developing world. Radical innovation invariably comes from marginal markets that reward ultra low-cost innovators.

■ Radical innovation often seems to come from outsiders to education who are not part of conventional thinking. A flow of outsider innovators into education is needed to challenge orthodoxy and introduce new ideas. That might come by opening up the way for new schools to be formed, such as Charter Schools. But other initiatives may work. Teach for America, for example, has spawned emulators around the world, which encourage talented young graduates to go into teaching for a couple of years immediately after leaving university. A version of that model could be adapted to innovation: finding ways for proven innovators to work on educational challenges.

■ Innovators are mixers: they blend together ideas and people to come up with new recipes. In high-technology fields much of this mixing takes place through networks and clusters: the classic example is Silicon Valley, which relies on a mixture of dense social networks to connect entrepreneurs, venture capitalists and universities, and the global connections of diaspora communities such as Indian software engineers. It is highly unlikely that a single location – a Silicon Valley for education– could play a similar role within the global education industry. But education will need its own versions of these clusters, probably many around the world, as places that innovators are drawn to.

■ Education systems will need much stronger skills in innovation management and leadership. Most training in education focuses on teaching, although in the last decade more emphasis has been put on leadership of schools and entire systems. Innovation, however, can seem risky because people in education have little experience of it and lack support to manage it. One solution might be to learn lessons from the success of the Indian Institutes of Technology in creating a cadre of highly entrepreneurial business technologists who span the United States and India. A Global Academy for Innovation in Education could start to gather and disseminate material to support innovators inside and outside education.

Innovators are mixers: they blend together ideas and people to come up with new recipes.

■ A vital part of that process will be to bring together innovators from education with those from technology. That already happens through conferences such as Online Educa and Learning Without Frontiers. Many of the leading technology companies such as Microsoft and Cisco have large education practices. Yet much of this innovation is led by technologists, pushing technology, rather than education innovators pulling it. It tends to come from centres of high technology in the United States rather than where the innovation is needed. One possibility would be to create a global programme of innovation camps, to bring together innovators and technologists, in the markets where the innovation is needed, to design effective solutions to common challenges. Coding and hacking camps are commonplace in the software industry. Some of those methods could be taken up to hack open the code for education.

■ Innovation thrives on customer insight, feedback and adaptation. In more fields users are becoming active partners in innovation as companies draw on their insights and ideas to develop and improve products. Companies as diverse as Dell, Starbucks, Intel, Apple, Muji and Lego have found ways to engage some of their consumers as partners in innovation. Many computer games thrive on adaptations added by users. The Tripadvisor service has transformed how travellers rate their experiences and alert one another to the merits of different places to stay and eat. John Hattie's extensive research shows that feedback between teacher and student is at the heart of effective learning. Education however seems not to be interested in the views of its direct consumers. There is a huge opportunity to create systematic ways for students to support innovation through rating their experiences and making suggestions for more effective approaches. In Nepal, the Rewrite the Future campaign helped to support more than

4,000 children's clubs, to give children a permanent voice in debates over education. This, with the help of the web, could become a much more widespread phenomenon.

■ Radical innovation in education will likely require financial innovation to fund it. New models of school and individual learning might well require new business models: from payment per lesson online to self-financing schools like Cristo Rey, to the free OpenCourseWare movement. New ideas get nowhere unless they can attract the right resources, at the right time. Independent funding, often from foundations, was vital to get most of our innovators started. More radical innovation will only come from more funding, dispersed more intelligently to promising projects. Education should learn lessons from the financial innovation that has mobilised resources to fight global warming and HIV, including carbon credits and bonds. Other innovations may play a role, such as linking education to microcredit and the Kiva platform through which individual donors in the developed world make investments in social ventures. Alongside raising additional funds for innovation, new skills would be needed to invest it wisely – new education social venture capitalists. Foundations such as the Bill and Melinda Gates Foundation and the MacArthur Foundation already have extensive knowledge about what makes for success as well as the pitfalls in this area, as do social venture funds such as Acumen in the United States and the National Endowment for Science, Technology and the Arts (NESTA) in the UK. More could be done to share these insights. One vehicle for this would be to create a model, global Education Social Venture Fund, with the explicit aim of developing truly game-changing innovations that could work for millions of learners. Another might be to create a small set of global innovation challenges – for example to radically improve literacy among girls, to increase the number of women teachers – and to orchestrate global competitions around those challenges.

■ At the end of the day, government will still be a vital player, especially in scaling up innovation. More research is needed to show how innovation within systems can be combined with innovation that comes from social pioneers outside the system. Our pioneers have found that a wide range of relationships are possible – they can act as providers, component-suppliers, partners, and programmers – for the larger system. This would be made much easier, however, if there were reliable and simple models to draw upon. If this were the case, then the relationship between government and social innovators, systems and movements, might become less fraught and more productive.

This might sound like an impossible wish list. But none of this involves doing anything that is not commonplace in another industry. Unless education systems can generate more successful radical innovations, then the gap between what people want and what the systems deliver will only grow.

That is because an irrepressible cultural change is afoot around the world. People are no longer prepared to be handcuffed to history, to be held back by where they come from. In millions of small ways all around the world boys and girls like Samet and Nasreen, Diego and Angelina are mutinying, refusing to accept their place in the social order in the old way. These children hope and expect their talent to be recognised and nurtured. They want more from life than their parents. If their hopes are disappointed then there will be a heavy price to pay.

Tove Wang, the instigator of Rewrite the Future, reflected on its success in getting better education to 10m children: "Parents are far more determined than governments to make sure their children get an education. They will go to extraordinary lengths to make sure their children get to school. If they are prepared to do that we should not let them down. It is not a miracle we did this. It is systematic, painstaking, hard work but you have to want it."

Children, parents, want more, different, better ways to learn. The question is whether the professionals in and around the education system want it too.

Detail of an office at Byrraju
Foundation, Bimasvaram

BIBLIOGRAPHY

■ GENERAL

Aldrich, R. (1982) *An Introduction to the History of Education.* London: Hodder and Stoughton.

Aldrich, R. (2006) 'Lessons from the History of Education: The Selected Works of Richard Aldrich.' London: Routledge.

Banerjee, A.V. and Duflo, E. (2011) *Poor Economics: A Radical Rethinking of the Way to Fight Global Poverty.* New York: PublicAffairs.

Barber, M. and Mourshed, M. (2007) 'How the World's Best Performing School Systems Come Out on Top.' McKinsey & Co.

Barber, M. and Mourshed, M. (2011) 'How The Best Schools Systems Keep Getting Better', McKinsey & Co.

Bryk, A.S., Bender Sebring, P., Allensworth, E., Luppescu, S. *Organizing Schools for Improvement: Lessons from Chicago.* Chicago, ILL: Chicago University Press.

Christensen, C. (1997) *The Innovator's Dilemma: When New Technologies Cause Great Firms to Fail.* Cambridge, MA: Harvard Business Press.

Christensen, C., Horn, M. and Johnson, C. (2008) *Disrupting Class: How Disruptive Innovation Will Change the Way the World Learns.* New York; London: McGraw-Hill Professional.

Claxton, C. (2008) *What's The Point of School?* Rediscovering the Heart of Education. Oxford: OneWorld.

Crutchfield, L.R. and McLeod Grant, H. (2008) *Forces for Good: The Six Practices of High-Impact Nonprofits.* San Francisco, CA: Jossey-Bass.

Darling-Hammond, L. (2010) *The Flat World and Education: How America's Commitment to Equity Will Determine our Future.* New York; London: Teachers College Press.

Dumont, H., Istance, D. and Benavides, F., eds. *The Nature of Learning: Using Research to Inspire Practice.* Paris: Educational Research and Innovation, OECD Publishing.

Friere, P. (2007) *The Pedagogy of the Oppressed.* London: Penguin Books.

Friere, P. (2007) *Education for Critical Consciousness.* New York: Continuum.

Fullan, M. (2010) *All Systems Go: The Change Imperative for Whole System Reform.* Thousand Oaks, CA: Corwin.

Gardner, H. (2011) *Truth, Beauty, and Goodness Reframed: Educating for the Virtues in the Twenty-First Century.* New York: Basic Books.

Hattie, J. (2009) *Visible Learning: A synthesis of over 800 meta-analyses relating to achievement.* London; New York: Routledge.

Levin, B. (2008) *How to Change 5000 Schools: A Practical and Positive Approach for Leading Change at Every Level.* Cambridge, MA: Harvard University Press.

Programme for International Student Assessment. (2010) *The High Cost of Low Educational Performance: The Long-Run Economic Impact of Improvements in PISA Outcomes.* Paris: Educational Research and Innovation, OECD Publishing.

Prahalad, C. (2008) *The Fortune at the Bottom of the Pyramid: Eradicating Poverty Through Profits, Enabling Dignity and Choice Through Markets.* Philadelphia: Wharton School Publishing.

Nussbaum, M.C. (1997) *Cultivating Humanity: a Classical Defense of Reform in Liberal Education.* Cambridge, MA; London: Harvard University Press.

Nussbaum, M.C. (2010) *Not for Profit: Why Democracy Needs the Humanities.* Princeton, N.J.: Princeton University Press.

Tooley, J. (2009) *The Beautiful Tree: A Personal Journey into How the World's Poorest People are Educating Themselves.* Washington, DC: Cato Institute.

Tyack, D. and Cuban, L. (1995) *Tinkering Toward Utopia: A Century of Public School Reform.* Cambridge, MA: Harvard University Press.

Wagner, T. (2008) *The Global Achievement Gap: Why Even Our Best Schools Don't Teach The New Survival Skills Our Children Need – And What We Can Do About It.* New York: Basic Books.

Willingham, D.T. (2009) *Why Don't Students like School?: A Cognitive Scientist Answers Questions about How the Mind Works and What it Means for the Classroom.* San Francisco: Jossey-Bass.

■ MORE DETAILED RESOURCES ON PARTICULAR ORGANISATIONS AND COUNTRIES

Abagi, O. and Odipo, G. (1997) 'Efficiency of Primary Education in Kenya: Situational Analysis and Implications for Educational Reform.' Discussion Paper DP 004/97. Nairobi: Institute of Policy Analysis and Research.

Baird, A. and Harrelson, W. (2008) *Analysis of Fundación Paraguaya's Financially Self-sufficient Agricultural High School: Documenting a Model of a Financially Self-sustaining School and the Opportunities and Challenges for Replication.* Washington, DC: Making Cents International for the Inter-American Development Bank.

Banerjee, A. et. al. (2005) *Remedying Education: Evidence from Two Randomized Experiments in India.* Cambridge, MA: National Bureau of Economic Research.

Banerjee, A. and Duflo, E. (2008) 'Addressing Absence.' Working Paper, MIT Poverty Lab. Cambridge, MA: MIT.

Barber, M. (2008) *Instruction to Deliver: Fighting to Transform Britain's Public Services.* London: Methuen Publishing Limited.

Barber, S.M. (2010) *Education Reform in Pakistan: This Time It's Going to be Different.* June. [presentation] Pakistan: Pakistan Education Task Force.

Bekman, S. (2000) *A Fair Chance: An Evaluation of the Mother and Child Education Program.* 2nd ed. Istanbul: Mother Child Education Foundation Publications.

Bekman, S. and Koçak, A.A. (2010) *Mothers Reporting: The Mother Child Education Program in Five Countries.* Istanbul: Mother Child Education Foundation Publications.

Boekaerts, M. 'The crucial role of motivation and emotion in classroom learning.' In: Dumont, H., Istance, D. and Benavides, F., eds. *The Nature of Learning: Using Research to Inspire Practice.* Paris: Educational Research and Innovation, OECD Publishing. Ch. 4.

Bunyi, G. (2006) 'Real Options for Literacy Policy and Practice in Kenya.' Literacy for Life, Education for All Global Monitoring Report. Paris: UNESCO.

Carson, S. (2010) 'Reflections on a Decade of Open Sharing: A New Generation of Web Resources. *MIT News,* [online] 20 December. Available at: http://web.mit.edu/newsoffice/2010/ocw-reflections-strang.html

Chaudhury, N. et. al. (2005) 'Provider Absence in Schools and Health Clinics'. *Journal of Economic Perspectives.*

Christensen, C.M., Horn, M.B. and Johnson C.W. (2010) *Rethinking Student Motivation: Why Understanding the 'Job' is Crucial for Improving Education.* Working Paper. Mountain View, CA: Innosight Institute.

Citizens Foundation, The. (2010). 'Light 1996-2010, Annual Report 2010'. Karachi: The Citizens Foundation.

Colbert, V. (2002) 'Improving Quality of Education for the Rural Poor: Escuela Nueva in Colombia.' In: de Moura Castro, C. and Verdisco, A., eds. *Making Education Work: Latin American Ideas and Asian Results.* Washington, DC: Inter-American Development Bank. Ch. 8.

Colbert, V. et al. (2008) *Escuela Nueva: Towards a New School for the XXIst Century: A Child Friendly School, International Prototype Kit Collection English Version.* Bogotá: Fundación Escuela Nueva Volvamos a la Gente.

Duflo, E., Dupas, P. and Kremer, M. (2004) 'Peer Effects, Pupil Teacher Ratios and Teacher Incentives: Evidence from a Randomised Evaluation in Kenya.' MIT Mimeo. Cambridge, MA: MIT.

Dumont, H. and Istance, D. (2010) 'Analysing and Designing Learning Environments for the 21st century.' In: Dumont, H., Istance, D. and Benavides, F., eds. *The Nature of Learning: Using Research to Inspire Practice.* Paris: Educational Research and Innovation, OECD Publishing. Ch. 1.

Furco, A. 'The Community as a Resource for Learning: an Analysis of Academic Service-learning in Primary and Secondary Education.' In: Dumont, H., Istance, D. and Benavides, F., eds. *The Nature of Learning: Using Research to Inspire Practice.* Paris: Educational Research and Innovation, OECD Publishing. Ch. 10.

Gandhi Kingdon, G (1999) 'School Participation in Rural India.' DEDPS No 18. London: Suntory and Toyota International Centres for Economics and Related Disciplines, London School of Economics.

Gandhi Kingdon, G. (2007) 'The Progress of School Education in India.' GPRG-WPS-071. Oxford and Swindon: Global Poverty Research Group and Economics and Social Research Council. See www.gprg.org

Ireland, T. (2007) 'Brazil: Non-formal Education.' Paris: UNESCO; also UNESCO (2007) 'Early Childhood Care and Education in Brazil.' Policy Review Report, Early Childhood and Family Policy Series. No. 13.

Istance, D. and Dumont, H. *'The Nature of Learning: Using Research to Inspire Practice.'* In: Dumont, H., Istance, D. and Benavides, F., eds. *The Nature of Learning: Using Research to Inspire Practice.* Paris: Educational Research and Innovation, OECD Publishing. Ch. 13.

Kearney, G.R. (2008) *More than a Dream: The Cristo Rey Story: How One School's Vision Is Changing the World.* Chicago, ILL: Loyola Press.

Lall, M.C. (2009) *Creating Agents of Positive Change - The Citizens Foundation in Pakistan.* Project Report. Pakistan: The Citizens Foundation.

McEwan, P.J. (1998) 'The Effectiveness of Multigrade Schools in Colombia.' *International Journal of Educational Development.* Vol. 19, No. 6, pp 435-452.

Medeiros Filho, B. and Galiano, M.B. (2005) *Neighbourhood as School: Mobilizing the Educational Potential of the Community/Barrio-Escuela: Movilizando el Potencial Educativo de la Comunidad.* São Paulo: Cidade Escola Aprendiz.

MIT OpenCourseWare. (2011) *Director Letter.* [online] Available at : http://ocw.mit.edu/about/director-letter/

Miyagawa, S. (2010) MIT 'OpenCourseWare: A Decade of Global Benefit.' *MIT Faculty Newsletter,* [online]. Vol XXIII, No. 1. Available at: http://web.mit.edu/fnl/volume/231/miyagawa.html

Moss Kanter, R. and Litow, S.S. (2009) *Informed and Interconnected: A Manifesto for Smarter Cities.* Working Paper 09-141. Cambridge, MA: Harvard Business School.

Neri, M. and Buchmann, G. (2007) 'Brazil Country Case Study.' Prepared for the Education for All Global Monitoring Report 2008. Paris: UNESCO. (2008/ED/EFA/MRT/PI/27).

Pratham (2005) 'Annual Status of Education Report, Pratham Resource Centre, Mumbai, 2005 and other years.' Mumbai: Pratham.

Ramachandran, V. et. al. (2005) 'Teacher Motivation in India.' Discussion paper. Bangalore: Azim Premji Foundation.

Schiefelbein, E. (2005) *Education and Employment in Paraguay: Issues and Perspectives.* Working Paper No. 2. Toronto, Canada: University of Toronto, Centre for International Studies – CADEP.

Schnieder, M. and Stern, E. (2010) 'The Cognitive Perspective on Learning: Ten Cornerstone Findings.' In: Dumont, H., Istance, D. and Benavides, F., eds. *The Nature of Learning: Using Research to Inspire Practice.* Paris: Educational Research and Innovation, OECD Publishing. Ch. 3.

Slavin, R.E. 'Co-operative Learning: What Makes Group-work Work?' In: Dumont, H., Istance, D. and Benavides, F., eds. *The Nature of Learning: Using Research to Inspire Practice.* Paris: Educational Research and Innovation, OECD Publishing. Ch. 7.

Wolfenden, F. (2008) 'The TESSA OER Experience: Building Sustainable Models of Production and User Implementation.' *Journal of Interactive Media in Education (2).*

Wolfenden, F., et al. (2010) 'Using OERs to Improve Teacher Quality: Emerging findings from TESSA.' In: Commonwealth of Learning, *Sixth Pan-Commonwealth Forum on Open Learning.* Kochi, India 24-28 Nov 2010.

APPENDIX

CASE STUDIES & LINKS

■ MAJOR CASES

**African Institute
for Mathematical Sciences**
www.aims.ac.za
—
Aprendiz
aprendiz.uol.com.br
—
Cristo Rey
www.cristoreynetwork.org
—
Escuela Nueva
www.escuelanueva.org
—
Fundación Paraguaya
www.fundacionparaguaya.org.py
—
Hole in the Wall
www.hole-in-the-wall.com
—
IMC Weekend School
www.imcweekendschool.nl
—
MIT OpenCourseWare
ocw.mit.edu
—
MOCEP
www.acev.org
—
Nanhi Kali
www.nanhikali.org
—
Pathways to Education
www.pathwaystoeducation.ca
—
Rewrite the Future
www.savethechildren.net/alliance/
what_we_do/rewritethefuture
—
Shafallah Center
www.shafallah.org.qa
—
TESSA
www.tessafrica.net
—
The Citizens Foundation
www.thecitizensfoundation.org
—
We Love Reading
www.welovereading.org

■ OTHER CASES MENTIONED

Al-Nayzak
www.alnayzak.org
—
Asociacion Ak'Tenamit
www.aktenamit.org
—
**The Bilingual Education Continuum
in Burkina Faso**
www.solidar.ch
—
Bridges to the Future
www.literacy.org
—
**British Open University's Digital
Education Enhancement Project**
www.open.ac.uk/deep/Public/web/
index.php
—
**College of Sustainability,
Dalhousie University**
sustainability.dal.ca/College_of_
Sustainab.php
—
The Connect Programme, Soliya
www.soliya.net/?q=connect_program
—
**The Distance Learning in the Amazon
Project**
www.seduc.am.gov.br
—
Education for Employment
www.efefoundation.org/homepage.html
—
EnviroProtect Biodiversity Programme
enviroprotect.i-strategis.net/en/tag/
biodiversity
—
Espacios para Crecer
www.devtechsys.com/projects/details/
combating-child-labor-dom
—
Gateway to the Future
view.fdu.edu/default.aspx?id=8575
—
Kalinga Institute of Social Sciences
www.kiss.ac.in
—
KOC Turkey Vocational Education
www.mesleklisesimemleketmeselesi
.com

MILLEE
www.cs.cmu.edu/~mattkam/lab/millee
.html
—
Neve Shalom/Wahal al-Salam School
www.nswas.com
—
Shine Centre
www.theshinecentre.org.za
—
**The Smallholders Farmers
Rural Radio Network**
smallholdersfoundation.org/index.html
—
**Tamer Institute for Community
Education**
www.tamerinst.org
—
The University for Peace, UN
www.upeace.org/UT
—
The 99
www.the99.org

**Qatar Foundation for Education,
Science and Community Development**
www.qf.org.qa
—
WISE-Qatar
www.wise-qatar.org

HIGH IMPACT INNOVATORS AT A GLANCE

PROJECT	PLACE OF ORIGIN	STAGE OF EDUCATION	INNOVATION	REACH / IMPACT
AIMS	South Africa	Postgraduate	Cross-disciplinary, collaborative, project-based pedagogy.	Plans for 10 centres graduating 800 per year.
Aprendiz	Brazil	School age	Community as a focus for learning alongside school.	Directly several thousands of children. Indirect influence on city and national policy.
The Citizens Foundation	Pakistan	School age	All female workforce to facilitate co-education.	Operates 730 schools serving 102,000 children.
Cristo Rey	US	Pre-college secondary	Financially self-sufficient school. Students work to earn money to pay for education.	Network of 24 schools, serving about 6,500 students.
Escuela Nueva	Colombia	Started in primary, spread to secondary	Self-organised, collaborative and independent learning organised around printed learning guides, allowing a single teacher to deal with many more children.	Methods used in more than 17,000 Colombian schools and taken up by seven other countries.
Hole in the Wall	India	School age	Self-organised and facilitated computer-based learning, mainly outside but also inside school.	500 computers installed serving perhaps millions of children.
MOCEP	Turkey	Pre-school	Trains groups of mothers to support one another to become early educators.	300,000+ mothers and children directly but also reshaped government early years policy.
MIT OpenCourseWare	US	University	Online, open access courseware.	72m unique users, spawned a global OpenCourseWare movement of more than 200 institutions.
Nanhi Kali	India	School-age girls	Special support programmes for girls to help them continue with education.	70,000 girls in eight states in India.
Pathways to Education	Canada	Pre-college secondary	Financial incentives and intensive mentoring to support the poorest students to learn.	16 sites running after school support for thousands of pupils from disadvantaged backgrounds.
Rewrite the Future	Norway/UK	School age	Building better schools, using alternative and accelerated pedagogy.	Improved education for 10m children in conflict zones.
Fundación Paraguaya	Paraguay	Late secondary school	Self-sufficient farm schools. Farm produce and tourism pay for education.	Three in Paraguay, several others in development in Latin America and Africa, global network of 2,000 self-sufficient education projects.
Shafallah Center	Qatar	0–21 yrs	Innovative mix of education, health and family support programmes for disabled children.	Global centre of excellence.
TESSA	UK/Africa	Teacher training	Modular open access, online learning platform for teacher training.	400,000+ African teachers.
The Weekend School	Netherlands	School age	Creative personalised learning projects to motivate children to learn, especially for immigrant communities.	Nine schools, mainly run on Sunday, 100 students each and 30 other copycat projects.
We Love Reading	Jordan	School age children	Training mothers to lead reading groups, using mosques, homes and community centres.	Four hundred mothers trained as reading coordinators. Rapid growth likely.

INDEX OF NAMES

A

Abdel Hadi, Rola 128
Acker, Carolyn 96*illus.*, 97, 122, 131
Acquino, Nilson 85, 86*illus.*, 87*illus.*
Afassinou, Komi 74–5*illus.*
African Institute for Mathematical Sciences (AIMS) 18, 25, 35–7*illus.*, 74*illus.*, 75*illus.*, 76*illus.*, 77*illus.*, 79, 116, 122, 132, 150
AIMS *see* African Institute for Mathematical Sciences (AIMS)
Al-Nayzak project (Palestine) 123
Ali bin Ali, Hassan 59
Ansari, Nasreen 62–3*illus.*, 152
Apple 132, 149
Aprendiz (Brazil) 34, 36–7*illus.*, 79, 113 15, 117, 117*illus.*, 118, 138, 150
Asociacion Ak'Tenamit (Guatemala) 89
Ataturk, Mustafa Kemal 80*illus.*

B

B.J. Cassin Foundation 122
Bandeirantes school (Brazil) 115
Banergee, Abhijit 98
Barber, Sir Michael 31, 140, 142
Bassett, Bruce 76
BBC Experiments 149
Bekman, Sevda 118, 122
Bhutto, Benazir 31
Bilingual Education Continuum (Burkina Faso) 57
Bill and Melinda Gates Foundation 122, 152
Boekaerts, Monique 98
Bridges to the Future 26, 52*illus.*
Brojas, Luizdary 20–1*illus.*
Bryk, Tony 142
Burt, Martin 84*illus.*, 85–6, 89, 116, 118, 122, 141

C

Caballero, Martina 86
Cape Town University (South Africa) 74
Carneiro Ribeiro Educational Centre (Brazil) 118
Castro, Marina 73
Centre for the Working Child (Peru) 121
Chan, Kalvin 97
Charter Schools (US) 139, 151
Chhapra, Mushtaq 31, 123, 138
Christensen, Clayton 98, 116
Colbert, Vicky 20–1*illus.*, 24, 73*illus.*, 118, 122, 140
College of Sustainability (Canada) 89
Colli, Cesar 118

Connect Programme, Soliya 89
Cristo Rey (United States) 34, 36–7*illus.*, 78*illus.*, 79, 98, 108, 118–9*illus.*, 121, 152
Crutchfield, Leslie R. 131
Cultivating Humanity (Nussbaum, 1997) 88

D

D'Oliveira, Cecelia 50–1, 54
Dajani, Rana 118, 130*illus.*, 140
Dar es Salam University 18
Darling-Hammond, Linda 25, 70, 79, 88
Dewey, John 73, 118
Digital Education Enhancement Project (UK) 52
Dimenstein, Gilberto 115
Distance Learning in the Amazon (Brazil) 51
Duflo, Esther 98

E

EARTH University (Costa Rica) 85
Edison, Thomas 116–17
Education for All Global Monitoring Report (2010) 57
Education for Employment 89–90
Egerton University (Kenya) 72
Elementary Education Act (UK, 1870) 138
Elurupadu village primary school (India) 60–1*illus.*
Engelbrecht, Chris 122
Ensuring Children Learn 63
Enviro-Protect (Cameroon) 89
Escuela Nueva (Colombia) 23–5, 34, 36–7*illus.*, 73–4, 79, 90, 108, 116, 118, 122, 131, 139, 140, 141, 148, 150
Espacios para Crecar (Dominican Republic) 57

F

Facebook 149
Fe y Alegría (Peru) 121
Flat World and Education, The (Darling-Hammond, 2010) 25, 70
Florentine, Hugo 86
Foley, Father John 121
Folha de Sao Paulo (newspaper) 115
Forces for Good (Crutchfield and McCleod Grant, 2008) 131
Ford, Henry 32
Freinet, Celestin 118
Freire, Paulo 118
Fullan, Michael 140, 142
Fundación Paraguaya (Paraguay) 34, 82–3*illus.*, 85, 108, 118, 122

G

Gardner, Howard 88
Gates, Bill 25
Gateway to the Future (United States) 57
General Motors 32
Goksel, Ayla 122, 139
Gollalakoderu village primary school (India) 64*illus.*
Google 149, 150
Green, Barry 77*illus.*, 141

H

Hahne, Fritz 74, 76*illus.*, 116, 123, 132
Hattie, Professor John 79, 90, 151
Hewlett Foundation 50
Hirsch, Eric Donald 88
Hole in the Wall (India) 35, 36–7*illus.*, 54–5*illus.*, 108, 132, 148, 150
How to Change 5000 Schools (Levin, 2008) 140
Hughes company 51
Hughes, David 97
Husseini, Aref 123

I

IMC Weekend School (the Netherlands) 34, 100-1*illus.*,102*illus.*, 122, 148, 150
Innovator's Dilemma, The (Christensen, 1997) 116
iTunes 149

J

JCEF (Education for Employment in Jordan) 90
Juvvalapalem primary school (India) 28–9*illus.*, 52*illus.*

K

K.C. Mahindra Educational Trust 62–3
Kalinga Institute of Social Sciences (India) 57
Kallakuru primary school (India) 26*illus.*, 28–9*illus.*, 52*illus.*, 64*illus.*
Kampala University 51
Karachi (Pakistan) 31
Kasese district (Uganda) 18
Khan Academy 141, 149
Kingdon, Geeta Ghandi 141
Kinyateke Primary School (Uganda) 18–9*illus.*
Korir, Paul Kibet 76
Kunskapsskolen (Sweden) 139

L

La Capilla (Colombia) 18, 20–1*illus.*, 146–7*illus.*
La Salle Brothers 85
Learning Neighbourhoods (Brazil) 115
Learning Without Frontiers 151
Levin, Ben 140, 142
Lillian, Eve 76, 77
Little Black Fish (Istanbul) 23
Living Light (United States) 89
Lutambi, Angelina 18, 20, 25

M

Madangir Resettlement Colony (New Delhi) 54
Makoko (Lagos) 141
Malineres, Jorge 85
Massachusetts Institute of Technology (Boston) 50*illus.*, 54, 131, 132, 141 *see also* OpenCourseWare (MIT)
MacArthur Foundation 152
McLeod Grant, Heather 131
Meta, Sheetal 62
Millennium Development Goals (UN) 24, 42
MIT OpenCourseWare *see* OpenCourseWare (MIT)
Mitra, Sugata 54, 132, 148
Mobile Immersive Learning for Literacy in Emerging Economies (MILLEE) 52, 60
MOCEP *see* Mother Child Education Program (MOCEP)
Model Schools programme (Byrraju Foundation) 28–9*illus.*, 52*illus.*
Modern School movement (France) 118
Montessori-style 23
Montessori, Maria 73
More Education programme (Brazil) 115
Mother Child Education Program (MOCEP) 23, 35, 79, 90, 116, 118, 122, 139, 140
Murray, Rick 121
Mutawa, Dr Naif 89

N

N.M. Joshi Municipal School (Mumbai) 133*illus.*
Naandi Foudation 63
Nakakawa, Juliet 76
Nanhi Kali (India) 35, 60, 62–3, 131, 133, 140
Nasser, Her Highness Sheikha Moza bint 32
National Endowment for Science, Technology and the Arts (NESTA) 152

National Institute of Teacher's Institute (Nigeria) 72
National University of Rwanda 76
Nike 132
Not for Profit (Nussbaum, 2010) 88
Nussbaum, Martha 88

■ O
Observatory School (South Africa) 57
Olcay, Muzzuz 22*illus.*, 23
100 Walls programme (Brazil) 115
Online Educa 151
Open University (UK) 36, 51, 72, 131, 149
OpenCourseWare (MIT) 34, 36–7*illus.*, 122, 132
OpenCourseWare Consortium 51
OpenStudy 51
Organizing Schools for Improvement (Byrk *et al.*) 142
Ozyegin, Aysen 118

■ P
Pakistan Education Task Force 31
Pathways to Education (Canada) 34, 94–98, 95*illus.*, 108, 122, 131, 140
Poddaer Mills (Mumbai) 65*illus.*
Poor Economics (Banerjee and Duflo, 2011) 98
Pratham (NGO, India) 24, 139, 140

■ Q
Qatar Foundation for Education, Science and Community Development 32
Qubbaj, Renad 116

■ R
Regent Park (Canada) 94–7
Rewrite the Future (Save the Children) 18, 34, 40–1*illus.*, 42, 44*illus.*, 45, 60, 64, 148, 152 *see also* Save the Children
Robinson, Sir Ken 88
Roeper School (Detroit) 121
Roeper, George and Annemarie 121
Rosenfeld, Marina 117*illus.*
Rowen, Norman 96*illus.*, 122, 131

■ S
Sagir, Azize 20, 22*illus.*, 23
Sagir, Samet 20–1*illus.*, 25, 152
San Francisco Agriculture School (Paraguay) 34, 82–3*illus.*, 84*illus.*, 85–7*illus.*, 98, 106–7*illus.*, 108
Save the Children 42, 45, 57, 79 *see also* Rewite the Future (Save the Children)

Seren, Ceren Can 20, 23
Shafallah Center (Qatar) 35, 36, 58–9*illus.*, 108, 118, 132, 141
Shine literacy programme (South Africa) 56*illus.*, 57
Singer, Helena 138*illus.*
Sita Ram Mill Compound School (India) 62–3*illus.*, 133*illus.*
Smallholders Farmers Rural Radio network (Nigeria) 54
Stellenbosch University (South Africa) 18, 74, 76
Strang, Gilbert 50–1

■ T
Tamer Institute (Gaza) 116
Tanzania 18
Teacher Education in Sub-Saharan Africa (TESSA) 35, 36–7*illus.*, 72, 77, 90, 108, 122, 131, 148
Teixeira, Anisio 118
Terwijn, Heleen 100, 100*illus.*, 102, 122, 148
TESSA *see* Teacher Education in Sub-Saharan Africa (TESSA)
The 99 (comic strip) 89
The Citizens Foundation (TCF) 31, 35, 42, 60, 79, 116, 122, 123, 131, 138, 139, 141
Thielman, Jeff 121
Thomas Jefferson High School for Science and Technology (Alexandria, USA) 151
Tooley, James 141
Turok, Neil 74, 116, 132
Twitter 150

■ U
UN University for Peace 89
UNESCO 24, 73
UNICEF 60, 72
United Kingdom elementary education 138
United States' elementary education 138–9

■ V
Valendra, Diego and Fabian 20–1*illus.*, 25, 152
Velaz, Father Maria 121
Visible Learning (Hattie, 2009) 90

■ W
Wagner, Professor Dan 52, 54
Wagner, Tony 88
Waiting for Superman (film) 25
Wang, Tove 42, 45, 64, 152

We Love Reading (Jordan) 35, 118, 126–7*illus.*, 128–9*illus.*, 130, 140
Weekend School *see* IMC Weekend School (the Netherlands)
Weisenberg, Maurita 57
Western Cape University (South Africa) 74
Why Don't Students Like School? (Willingham, 2009) 100
Wikipedia 149
Willingham, Daniel 100
WISE *see* World Innovation Summit for Education (WISE)
WISE Awards scheme 32
WISE Prize for Education 32
Wolfenden, Freda 72
World Absenteeism Survey (World Bank) 24
World Bank *see* World Absenteeism Survey (World Bank)
World Health Organization (WHO) 59
World Innovation Summit for Education (WISE) 25, 32

■ Y
YouTube 50–1, 141, 149, 150